THE COMPLETE
SHETLAND SHEEPDOG

Margaret Norman

Howell Book House

HOWELL
BOOK
HOUSE

New York

HOWELL BOOK HOUSE
A Simon & Schuster / Macmillan Company
1633 Broadway
New York, NY 10019

MACMILLAN is a registered trademark of Macmillan, Inc.

ISBN 1-58245-043-9

Library of Congress Cataloging-in-Publication Data
available on request

Manufactured in Singapore

10 9 8 7 6 5 4 3 2 1

636. 737

This book is dedicated to the memory of
Beryl M. Herbert.

Francehill Gold Venture.

*A*CKNOWLEDGEMENTS

James Norman for all that typing! Jean Haslett for a lot of patient photography, and Derek Smith for his help over photo selections. Tony Bridge for help over the internet. Gerald and Mary Fallas for help over 'the origins'. To all friends and fellow breeders for supplying photographs.

CONTENTS

1 INTRODUCING THE SHELTIE

It was love at first sight – my affair with the Shetland Sheepdog started long ago, when I was a child. Going to school on the bus, I saw a silver-haired man standing at the side of the road, waiting to cross. He had six beautiful little dogs with him. Sitting on the back seat with my two older sisters, I was able to twist round and watch the dogs until the bus went on its way and that beautiful vision was out of sight. I could hardly wait until the next morning – and sure enough he – and they – were there!

It was not long until we were waving to each other and one day the temptation was too great and I slipped off the bus and spoke to my hero. He told me he was Colonel Russell and that these dogs were Shelties – this was the start of my love affair with the breed.

The bus had driven off – and I had to chase after it to school, much to the annoyance of my long-suffering sisters. As can be imagined, my home-coming was full of my meeting and, like most children, I was putting pressure on my parents for them to allow me to visit my new friend. When the weekend came my father agreed to cycle with me to the house, and, after human introductions, we were then introduced to the dogs – what joy!

I was then told that Colonel Russell

Margaret Norman pictured with her first Sheltie.

6

The ideal family companion: Ch. Myriehewe Rosa Bleu with Robert Powley.
Photo: Russell Fine Art.

wanted a pet home for a blue merle dog that was going to grow far too big for show purposes. I looked pleadingly at my father. I had to wait a whole week before I could collect Sky Blue of Crawley-Ridge, and though he was not the founder of my Francehill line, he certainly was the dog that introduced me to the dog scene. There was no sitting down and writing lists of dos and don'ts – it was literally love at first sight!

THE RIGHT CHOICE
When buying a pedigree (purebred) dog, it is sensible to choose one that suits your household. The Sheltie to me

has everything – he is the right size, big enough to be hardy and enjoy country walks, but small enough to be tucked under your arm in an emergency – and certainly small enough to sit on your lap. The breed is currently in the working group, as recognised by the UK Kennel Club, but is due to move to the herding group in 1999, where it is already categorised by the American Kennel Club. This means that the breed should be hardy, not needing frequent veterinary visits, and intelligent, which Shelties certainly are. It is sad that the breed used to have a reputation for nervousness, and if breeders have not improved much else, they can certainly take a well-earned pat on the back for improving this characteristic. I would say that the Sheltie today is as sound in temperament as most other breeds.

AN IDEAL PET

One of the misconceptions that people have is that Shelties need lots of exercise – they do not. They love walks, they love freedom and they love country life, but give them a choice of all that or being with their owner, then every Sheltie I have had anything to do with will value their owner's company above all else! There is no need to pity the Sheltie who is an old person's pet – that constant cuddling on the lap is paradise, and even though exercise may be less than ideal, the advantages outweigh the disadvantages.

As a child's pet they are also ideal, although I would urge parents not to let the long-suffering little Sheltie be pulled about by excited toddlers. I can well remember my own children giving a lot of companionship to our Shelties – culminating in having their own dog when we thought them sensible enough.

Shelties are the perfect family dog – their loyalties lie with their owners. Those ears miss nothing, either! The slightest sound will alert their attention, and the breed is known not for its guarding qualities but for letting you know when strangers are about. They are good mixers, but on the whole I do not think they socialise readily with other breeds. I know that on entry to a show they spot another Sheltie before we can – and the tail wags on recognition. It is almost as if there is a secret Sheltie society.

The very versatile nature of the breed is one of its charms; as a family pet they excel, and the intelligence of the breed is visible. They are easy to train, and in fact many Shelties are trained for Obedience and Agility competition with excellent results.

The versatile Sheltie: Charles and Polly from Mountmoor are excellent sailing companions. Photo: Ferguson.

2 ORIGINS OF THE SHELTIE

Much has been written about the Sheltie and its origins. It sounds almost romantic to say that they were little Toonie or Peerie dogs from the Shetland Isles of Scotland, and it is not in doubt that diminutive dogs of roughly Collie appearance existed there, but how had they evolved as the crofter's friend? Money was scarce and existence was meagre in the Shetland Isles. There would be no room for the larger working Collie, and it would require more food than a smaller dog. The little dog that evolved into the Sheltie probably has a background as mixed as any street mongrel!

We all like to think of our dogs as 'highly pedigree', but of course all dogs started off with the purpose of being useful to their human masters. If there was an indigenous dog to the Islands, it has probably had such an infusion of different blood that no-one can say for certain whether it started out as a small sheepdog or as a guard and companion. Whatever the original intention, my thoughts are that the little dog was selected for his intelligence, quickness and versatility.

JACK OF ALL TRADES

Early photographs show a black dog, small in size and bearing little resemblance to the present-day Sheltie. The little dog found in the Shetland Isles seems to have been a utilitarian chap, used as a guard and sheepdog by the crofters, who were earning a meagre living with their few sheep and small strips of land. Life must have been hard, so the dog would have to be small, with an appetite to match. He would also have to be versatile, as he would need to be able to look after the few sheep sustainable on the small strips of land. Shetland sheep are a small breed, and the Sheltie would need to be nimble and intelligent. He would also be a useful guard, and although his size would not act as a deterrent, his extra alertness and keen hearing would help to guard the crofters' wives, who would probably be busily working on their weaving and knitting.

It seems that the little Sheltie was a jack of all trades, able to herd the sheep, guard the croft and be a general helpmate. He had to be small, as there were no such luxuries as tinned dog food or complete diets in those days!

WIDER INTEREST

It was probably in the nineteenth century that people started recognising and taking an interest in the little Sheltie. It is noted that Sir Walter Scott, the Scottish romantic poet and novelist, admired the diminutive little sheepdogs, and they have had several admirers, including the British Navy. I understand that at the turn of the century, several Shelties found themselves purchased and taken to the British mainland. This must have added another string to the crofters' bow, and the prices paid for the dogs must have seemed very tempting when they and their families were existing on a shoestring!

STANDARDISING THE BREED

At the turn of the century there was interest in the Sheltie as a possible show dog. At first they were referred to as

The Shetland Sheepdog was originally used for herding, and the working instinct is still retained, as demonstrated in this American herding test. Photo courtesy: Dr. Rebecca Golatzki.

Ch. Woodvold: Bred by Keith & Ramsey, owned by Miss Thynne.

Shetland Collies, but some of the Collie breeders were appalled to think that the name of the Collie was being used to name these little black dogs, and in due course the name was amended to the Shetland Sheepdog.

The first breed club was the Scottish Shetland Sheepdog Club, formed in 1909, and it is in fact in Scotland that the breed started to take shape. Several breeders set out to standardise the type, and Mr Logie started producing some good specimens under the Lerwick prefix, as did Mr Thompson of the Inverness kennels. It is pure conjecture what would have happened if Rough Collie blood had not been added – the Rough Collie was quite established at this time, and there is absolutely no doubt that the present day Sheltie owes a great deal to the introduction of this Collie blood. Our breed type is approximately of Rough Collie in miniature – many of the early kennels proudly advertised their stock as such. Today, we frown on the description, but no-one can argue that the breed owes a lot to the introduction of Collie blood, and to the foresight of those early breeders.

Shelties started to appear in the show ring, and in 1906 some were exhibited at no less a show than Crufts, though it seems that they were mainly shown in Scotland. Although Scotland had put so much into the development of the breed and had started to schedule them at their shows, which were surprisingly well-supported, the first Challenge Certificate was awarded in 1915 not at a Scottish show, but in Birmingham, England, to Frea, who was by Lerwick Jarl.

The breed had many admirers across

Ch. Hurly Burly: An early Champion bred by Mr Hurrell, owned by Miss M. Grey.

the Atlantic, and the first exports from the Scottish mainland occurred in the 1920s and 1930s.

THE GENETIC LEGACY
The Collie crosses carried out in these early years undoubtedly helped to achieve that look of quality – bearing in mind that our little Toonie or Peerie friend from the Shetland Isles was nothing more than a mongrel.

Despite the importance of the Collie influence, no doubt the fact that size is still a problem can be levelled at the Collie influence! The present-day Sheltie unfortunately shows a big variation in height. We have all tried to standardise size in our various strains, but still that big one crops up, as, in fact, does that little one. The bigger ones must be 'throwbacks' to the days when the early breeders openly crossed

the little mongrel from the Shetland Isles with Collies to improve the type and appearance.

Size is not the only problem, as gay, curling tails can still also crop up, probably due to Pomeranian blood, or some of the attractive little Spitz breeds that were – and are still – prevalent in Scandinavia.

When I first started showing it was quite common to see a 'Yakki' mask, although it is less common today. This is where the face is plain, and a black (or at least heavily shaded) mask is evident, without a white blaze, which comes from the Collie influence. On puppies, a Yakki mask is much exaggerated, and your pup can have a face which is marked in a similar way to a present day Keeshond or Norwegian Buhund. It is not a fault, and in fact several Champions were made that had

*Ch. Kilravock Nettle: Owned
and bred by Miss Thynne.*

a Yakki mask. I understand that the Yakki dog was a native of Iceland, and it is perfectly possible that some of these dogs came to the Shetland Islands with whaling expeditions or fishing trips, and the little Island dogs must have been crossed with them.

So it can be said that our little Sheltie owes his origins in part to an indigenous dog from the Scottish Islands, mixed with various Romeos from Scandinavia or Iceland, until recognition at the early part of the 1900s – and then the deliberate introduction of Rough Collie, so by the time World War I broke out our Sheltie was being recognised as a pretty little show dog with working qualities.

*A well-grown puppy from the fifties
showing the shaded 'yakki' mask
typical of that era.
Photo: Ella Harker.*

3 CHOOSING YOUR SHELTIE

We have established that Shelties are a working breed, but they are also very adaptable, and one of the nicest things about them is that they love being with people. They are perhaps not over-effusive with strangers, but they are totally loyal to their owners. If we could see inside our Shelties' minds I think they would much prefer to live in close proximity to their owners than in the most luxurious home where human contact is low.

Having decided that the Sheltie is the breed you want, you need to have a family get-together to establish exactly what you are looking for.

MALE OR FEMALE
If you already have a dog, then it would be sensible to have another of the same sex. Do you have children? It might be prudent to have a dog, not a bitch – it would be awful if someone let the bitch out when she was in season!

Whether you choose a dog or a bitch is entirely personal. I would recommend a male puppy in most cases. Sheltie males are not likely to chase after the neighbour's bitch, or to mount the children! A bitch, on the other hand, will come into season at least once a year – and then after a season she will shed her entire coat. I hate the thought of bitches being spayed automatically, and personally I would prefer not to sell a bitch puppy into a home where she was going to be neutered as a matter of course.

SIZE
Are you drawn to the bigger Sheltie, or do you want a little one? We, as breeders, all try to breed the correct size, but often nature sends us a large 'throwback' which can grow almost to Collie size, which is no use to you if you want a tiny one. Tell the breeder exactly what you want.

COAT

The fact that the Sheltie is long-coated is a plus in my book, as I like a dog to be 'covered' – but if you hate grooming, or are extra fussy about your carpets getting covered in hair, then perhaps they are not the breed for you.

Most pet owners like a white collar, and some people want a white blaze up the face. I have had requests for all sorts of things, and, no doubt like all other breeders, I try to avoid disappointing the new owner. For show prospects, the markings are relatively unimportant – the size and conformation of the dog are what matter. However, when people are looking for a pet puppy, often the markings are extremely important. I often wonder if the popularity of 'Lassie', with her white collar, has something to do with this. A white collar is glamorous, but not essential on a show specimen.

PET OR SHOW

Another very important point to consider is just exactly what do you want from your Sheltie. Is he to be the family pet? If so, tell the breeder that show points are not as important as character. Do you want him to train for obedience or agility? If so, choose one from a strain that is well-known for temperament. Do you want a show dog? This sounds easy, but, like all breeders, we are not keen to sell that pick of the litter puppy to a beginner – so much can go wrong. If you want to enter the world of dog shows, then set your sights lower on your first dog, as you will have a lot to learn. Explain all this to the breeder – the last thing they will want is to see a substandard exhibit in the ring bearing their prefix. Perhaps you already own Shelties, but fancy an addition to your stock to give you an influx of new blood. Choose wisely.

When choosing a Sheltie as a pet you can not do better than to place yourself in the hands of a reliable breeder. A puppy of pet quality crops up as often, or more often, as a show prospect.

Ch. Shelridge Sunflower (Sametri Sunkelp at Shelridge – Stationhill Corn Dolly). Bred and owned by Mrs Aaron. The sable colour can range from pale gold to deep mahogany.

FCI Int. Ch. Francehill Mi'Lord (Ch. Cultured At Cashella – Francehill Fortune Teller Of Lochkaren). Bred by Mrs M. Norman, owned by Martina Feldhoff. Tricolours are black on the body with rich tan markings.

Photo: Feldhoff.

Ch. Francehill Willow Pattern (Donax Troop The Colour At Rivvalee – Francehill Mystery). Blue merle is a clear silvery blue, splashed and marbled with black.

Photo: Haslett.

Funnily enough, Shelties are easy and trouble-free as pets, but as show dogs their future is fraught with problems. Anyone who thinks Shelties are an easy breed to 'run on' for exhibition should think again – and then again!

THE OLDER DOG

If you are not in a position to house train a young puppy, then why not consider giving a home to a rescued Sheltie? Occasionally, a dog or bitch will need re-homing. This, in all probability, is not the fault of the dog; there are many reasons why dogs end up in rescue centres. A list of breed clubs is given at the back of the book, and most of these run rescue schemes. You may just be lucky and be able to offer a home to one of their dogs.

Being such a gentle little dog, it is not often that Shelties need re-homing, but the unexpected can happen to any family; death, divorce and ill health can all result in a little Sheltie needing a new home. You will be thoroughly assessed by the rescue centre, as they will want a successful result, rather than have the dog passed from one home to another. Be prepared to give a donation too!

FINDING A BREEDER

If you decide you want a puppy, the first thing that you need to do is to find a breeder, so you can visit and see Shelties in their home environment. Do not be tempted to answer that advertisement in the local paper – be sensible. The puppy is going to cost the same, whether from a reputable breeder, a pet owner or a puppy farm. In the last case, the puppies were probably bought to resell, and the puppy farm owner probably does not know or care anything about the mother, the father, or the rearing of this specialist breed. It is not as easy as we suppose to find a good breeder – where do you start?

The best way to set the ball in motion is to write to your national Kennel Club. They will reply with a list of breeders, or, if you ask about clubs within the breed, they will furnish either a list of breed clubs or mention

It is helpful if you can see close family relations when you view a litter. This is Zygotes Golden Boy with his six puppies.

Photo: Feldhoff.

Sheltie puppies are irresistable, so you need to keep a cool head when assessing the litter.

one that is in your area.

Another way of getting in touch is to go to a dog show – sit and watch the judging, and when the time is appropriate, speak to the person who has been showing a dog that has taken your fancy. Most breeders are very good at referring you to other breeders if they have no puppies themselves.

ASSESSING THE LITTER

It is important to see as many of the litter as you can (some may have gone by the time you get there), and not only seeing the mother, but seeing her with her puppies.

The sire is often not on the premises, as perhaps the breeder will have decided to use an outside stud dog, and he could be owned by someone living miles away. Try to see a photograph of him if you can.

It is absolutely pointless to ask the breeder for a pet if you want a show dog. It can be extremely annoying to sell a puppy in good faith as a pet, only to hear that it was later at a show. If you want a show puppy, then be absolutely up front and tell the breeder your requirements and how experienced you are as an exhibitor.

CHOOSING A SHOW PUPPY

Choosing a puppy for the show ring is a complicated business and after half a century's experience, I can still get this

It is important to see as many members of the litter as possible. Photo: Piet Jongepier.

wrong. The obvious answer would be to choose as late as possible, but this is totally impossible if you are buying-in a puppy – the breeders may well decide to keep the best for themselves, which is their prerogative. Also, if the puppy is for sale and you hesitate, he may well have been sold by the time you eventually ring to say that you have decided to buy that little puppy that appealed to you last week. Be decisive and go with your first impressions.

When asked what is the best age to select that pick of litter the obvious answer is 11 months and three weeks! Most breeders like puppies to start leaving at around seven or eight weeks. This age is ideal, as there is no stress

THE SHOW PUPPY
Photos: Haslett.

At ten weeks of age, this puppy is showing good overall balance.

The head should be wedge-shaped, and the ear carriage should be alert.

The forelegs must be straight when viewed from the front.

In profile, the head should show a definite stop and level head planes. Note the good underjaw.

involved, whereas at four or five months, the little fellow is developing a brain box and trauma can set in at the sudden change in his environment. At seven weeks, it is apparent how the puppy features in the litter – to be safe, it is always better to go for one in the middle. Often, the smallest is fine-boned and can be 'Pommie' in type, though this advice is given as a guide, not a rule. The biggest in the litter will invariably grow too big. It is so disheartening to select one that is a 'grower'. By the time he is four months old he may well develop big knees and feet, a longer muzzle and back – in general, he will be of Collie 'type'.

As a guide, the promising puppy will weigh about 4lbs at seven weeks, according to how well-reared they are. Even at this age, the puppy should have an air of quality. The head must be filled up – anything snipey-muzzled will probably develop a long, fine foreface: the muzzle must not look like a beak. Check that the eyes are not full and forward facing: eyes should be almond-shaped and set obliquely, and must be expressive, giving a sweet look.

It is important that the puppy has a chin; so many Shelties fail in this respect, and the lips should meet. Look to see that the teeth are scissor-bite. Occasionally a level bite will grow right, but when there is a gap between the top incisors and lower incisors, then this will only become more pronounced as the puppy grows. Never hope that an overshot mouth will come right, because it will not!

Sheltie ears can behave in the most extraordinary way, and this can be very alarming. In a perfect world the ears should be fairly small and carried well up on the head, with the tips facing forward. If the ears are large in size and set low on the head, then be careful. Heavy, low-set ears are much harder to cope with than ears that prick up.

The puppy should have a neck of sufficient length to be able to carry the head proudly, and this is perfectly detectable even in a puppy. The front, even at this young age, should be straight. Shoulder angulation should be felt for; an upright forearm at this stage will not grow into good angulation later. The topline must be visibly straight and level; anything longcast will either grow too large or have one of those long, dippy backs that are to be avoided. The hindquarters must be angulated; the stifle, even at this age, should have some shape to it and the hocks must be low and sturdy.

Tails are a law unto themselves. Feel to check that it is not set on high. A highset tail will almost always be carried high, but do not be alarmed to see the whole litter playing with their tails up – or, even worse, curling around. Check the set of the tail; if it is lowset, then there is every chance that it will end up being carried properly. I hate to see gay tails, and I am often amazed that tails carried gaily are tolerated in several countries abroad – but to most breed specialists it is a taboo.

All puppies have a 'puppy-fluff' coat. If you examine its density, I suggest it to be a fair assumption that those with long guard hairs grow the most profuse coats, whilst those that are less fluffy end up with what is known as a 'fitting jacket'.

In today's show ring it is expected that each exhibit has the temperament to stand up to the rigours of showing. While we do not necessarily expect a showing statue, it is reasonable to expect a dog not to show nervousness in the show ring. I am convinced that temperament and showmanship are points to be bred for. Choose your show prospect with this in mind – anything that vanishes under the table, or trembles with nerves when being handled, is to be avoided like the plague.

Bearing all these points in mind, when you have chosen your puppy, be positive and try not to listen to too much advice from alternative sources.

Where price is concerned, it might be prudent to ring round a few breeders to compare prices, but on no account should you try to barter with the breeder. Buying a puppy is a privilege, and friendship will probably develop between you and the breeder. I know that I like to keep in touch with everyone who has bought one of my babies, and no doubt other breeders do too.

When I first started I was fortunate to be given a bitch puppy on breeding terms – this actually meant that I paid a small sum, and eventually arranged to give back four puppies, two from each of the first two litters. It worked for me and the breeder who took the risk with me, but I must say that I have heard of several disasters with breeding terms and my advice would be to purchase outright whenever possible.

PREPARATION
You will need to get organised to welcome your new family member.

BEDS AND BEDDING
With a new puppy I see no sense in

There is no need to buy an expensive bed. A cardboard box will make a comfortable bed for the first few weeks. Photo: Lloyd Owen

buying it an expensive bed – they usually get chewed. A strong, clean cardboard box is just as good – it costs nothing and can be changed when it gets grubby. Put a layer of newspaper inside the box, and then a warm blanket – the invention of fleecy nylon blankets has been a blessing; it is always cosy and so easily washed. As well as this, the puppy will need something to cuddle up to – try knotting an old woollen vest or small jersey; just something of yours to bring a little comfort if needed. After he has passed the chewing stage he can progress to a smart bed – but for the first six months at least, save your money.

CRATES

If you travel around, or have some valuable carpets, why not consider buying a crate? Some years ago it was considered taboo to put a 'working' breed into one of those prisons! However, I can honestly say that I would be lost without my crate. You can buy fold-up crates of varying sizes; they have a rigid plastic floor and you can supply a piece of fleecy nylon blanket to the exact size of the base. I get my puppies accustomed to going in a crate right from the start – they are safe and your carpets are safe! It has been proved that they are the most secure form of travel for your dog. My dogs will happily go into their crate and the reward of a chew will encourage this.

GROOMING EQUIPMENT

The first brush you will need is just a teaching brush, soft and small in size. When the coat is progressing you can purchase a better brush – Mason Pearson brushes are marvellous. Two combs will be needed: a small one with teeth fairly close together, and one large one with the teeth well separated. This will be used to rake out dead coat and is invaluable. I thoroughly recommend that you buy your own nail clippers; it is so easy to clip your dog's nails and you should use them on a regular basis.

With modern-day feeding it is essential that your puppy learns to have his teeth cleaned. If this is done regularly, you will need a medium bristle brush and a tube of special dog toothpaste – these have a meaty taste and will not taste unpleasant to the young chap.

COLLAR AND LEAD

The collar purchased for the new puppy will be a temporary one. It must be tight enough to prevent it from being pulled off over his head, but soft enough not to irritate him. The lead must be light – anything heavy will impede lead training.

TOYS

Any toys you provide must be the cuddly sort. If any of the toys have button eyes, these must be removed for safety. Do not give your puppy

anything he might swallow, such as small balls.

COLLECTING YOUR PUPPY

You will have arranged a collection day with the breeder. It is important that you are organised for this because it may be the puppy's first introduction to the car. I actually get my own puppies used to the sound and smell of the car before this big day, but there is no reason why the breeder you have bought your puppy from should have done this. If possible, try to take someone with you for the very good reason that this new puppy must enjoy his first car ride – a lot depends on it. If you are on your own it will probably be sensible to take a crate or box and make

sure he is safely shut in to avoid him distracting you from your driving! Now, bearing in mind that he is leaving his mother and siblings, who have been at the centre of his world until now, it is understandable that he will voice his disapproval at being shut in on his own, no doubt getting himself stressed to the point of being travel sick! How much nicer to have someone to accompany you, who will sit in the front seat with a clean (but old) towel on their lap, and the new baby safely sitting on the towel. There is no need to keep fussing him, just treat it as an everyday occurrence and he will travel accordingly. This first trip in the car will probably set the pattern for his travelling behaviour for the rest of his life. Just in case he should be sick, it would be sensible to arm yourself with some kitchen roll. If you have a long journey, it is better not to let the puppy out in the vain hope that he will relieve himself. He probably will not, and remember that you two are only acquaintances as yet, so he will not heed your voice.

PAPERWORK
You should receive a copy of your puppy's pedigree, Kennel Club registration and transfer documents and the diet sheet.

DIET SHEET
The food as recommended on your diet sheet is a must! The breeder will have given you a diet sheet and my advice is to stick to it absolutely. Even if well meaning people advise other foods,

stick to the diet sheet. It is important that your puppy's tummy stays right – he should be passing firm, dark stools, and anything that produces loose, light-coloured faeces must not be fed. If in doubt, seek expert advice.

ARRIVING HOME
Much will depend on how long a journey you have had, but the usual rule upon arriving home is to welcome the new family member with a small meal. Look at the diet sheet, and whichever meal is nearest to the time of your arrival home, then offer him this. Usually, the most important thing for the puppy is to explore, and he will often go from place to place with that innocent inquisitiveness that always appears as if he is checking that everything is up to his standard! If he has eaten some food, the next step is to take him outside, but it is no use just putting him out – take five minutes yourself to amble around the garden with him. Do not forget to praise him if he spends his penny, but if he does not, bring him in and put newspaper down inside the doorway. Just like a baby, he will want a nap after all the excitement of the journey and the subsequent exploration, so have his bed ready.

INTRODUCING THE FAMILY
If you have other dogs or animals, a great deal depends on this first introduction. Try not to make too big a 'thing' of it. Perhaps the other dogs

Allow your puppy to explore his new surroundings.
Photo: Lloyd Owen.

could have gone with you to the kennels to collect the new puppy, in which case they would have had a chance to say 'hello' to each other. If not, then maybe you could let the other dogs into the garden and bring the puppy straight to them, putting him down as if it is the most normal thing in the world, making rather more fuss of the present family members than of the puppy. After the initial sniffs, they usually accept each other without challenge. Try to avoid the scenario of picking the puppy up and being too timid to let the other dogs sniff him, and definitely do not push him into their faces, as this might incite needless resentment. Remember that dogs are far nicer than humans and seldom suffer from jealousy!

THE FIRST NIGHT

There are two ways of looking at the settling-in process. Should you start as you mean to go on and ignore any whimpers, or do you feel sympathy for the puppy, away from its siblings for that first night, and allow him to sleep with you to make up for that sudden feeling of being alone? As a breeder, I suppose I should opt for the former approach and ignore his pleas, but I do have sympathy for the puppy – alone and probably feeling a little lost. You can help to get him off to sleep by providing a hot water bottle, well wrapped and tucked under the blankets of his bed, or you can provide a 'chew', and hope that this will amuse him until he is drowsy. I have heard the suggestion of providing a ticking clock as a comforter, but knowing my puppies I can imagine them chewing off the winding knobs!

So, your approach is up to you – I am more inclined to favour the 'softly-softly' attitude – it is a big world and it is horrid to suddenly wake up alone. Would it be impossible to take your puppy upstairs with you? Otherwise, the kitchen is the most popular place for a new puppy to sleep and settle into the household. If you bought a crate, this could make a little portable bedroom.

SUMMING UP

To sum up, your needs for your new Sheltie puppy will be:
The food as recommended on the diet sheet.
A small, soft collar and light lead.
A fleecy blanket and a soft cuddly item.
A light brush, two combs and nail clippers.
A medium-bristle toothbrush and dog toothpaste.
A crate (optional)
Do not forget that store of old newspapers!

4 CARING FOR YOUR SHELTIE

Buying a dog is a commitment not to be taken lightly. Shelties are sensitive and highly intelligent. How often I have heard people say "I don't know what I would do without the dogs", and I must say that at times of stress or sadness Shelties have this wonderful knack of knowing your mood. With a friend this perceptive it is only reasonable to look after him to the best of your ability. Look after, not spoil! He will need companionship, exercise, balanced food and some training. The Sheltie that lives in a sumptuous home, but alone all day is to be pitied, but the dog that has a poorer home but his owner's companionship is to be envied.

HOUSE TRAINING
The first introduction to your home for your new puppy will set the pattern for his learning abilities. My puppies are trained to relieve themselves on

Ch. Edglonian Rocking Robin: Providing the correct care is the key to owning a happy, healthy dog. Photo: Pearson.

newspapers, and for them the fact that the newspapers are by the back door means that they soon learn that to pop down outside earns them some cooing praise. I cannot emphasise too strongly that Shelties respond to 'praise and reward' training and house training is no exception. Common sense will tell you that every time the puppy wakes from a sleep he will automatically relieve himself, so forestall this by taking him into the garden as soon as he wakes up, amble slowly with him until the deed is done, then be enthusiastic in your praise. Also after meals he will want the same attention. By all means chastise with a firm "No" if a mess is made, you have to let him know that indoors is "No" in a firm voice but outside is "Clever boy" in a cooing voice.

Try not to be anxious over house training – I would say on average that by four months the idea should be in place; perhaps, to be realistic, we would expect a puppy to be clean by six months of age. There is no need to write to the author with news that your puppy has never had 'an accident' indoors because I can well remember times when this has been true of my own puppies.

A well-balanced diet is essential during the vital growing period. Photo: Haslett.

DIET

All dogs vary, but on the whole I find that Shelties need a high protein diet. Mine do well on canned puppy food, chopped beef, or some of the dry puppy foods; personally I prefer these fed soaked rather than fed dry.

The breeder will have provided a diet sheet and it is very important to stick to this – a puppy's stomach can be easily upset, and house training is much easier if you are cleaning up a nice firm stool! The puppy's stomach is small and for this reason we like to feed small but frequent meals. Our own puppies have five meals a day between five weeks and four months of age. I have found that every litter varies, but on average the first meal of the morning is canned puppy food, the second meal is dry puppy diet which has been soaked so there are no sharp edges, the third meal is puppy weaning porridge, the fourth meal is a repeat of the early morning canned meat, and the last meal of the

day is a repeat of the previously soaked puppy kibble. Many friends and fellow-breeders will have different feeding methods – many breeders feed an 'ad lib' dry kibble system with good results. I can say that most UK breeders follow the same sort of system as I do and my puppies reflect the care given to them.

It is impossible to give quantities because Shelties can vary in size, but my advice for feeding is to be generous. I do like to see fat, chunky puppies – the start of their lives is all-important. As your puppy grows, so his appetite will stabilise. On average I would suggest five meals a day until the puppy is four months old, then stop the midday puppy weaning porridge; then at six months stop the second morning meal, and by nine months the second afternoon meal can be dropped. This leaves the first meal of the day at breakfast and the second main meal in the afternoon. My own adult dogs enjoy two meals, dry high-protein kibble in the morning, and for the main meal in the afternoon they have high-protein complete food of the flaked variety, moistened with water, light stock or sometimes skimmed milk, and to this I add at least two tablespoons of top quality tinned meat. Sometimes I will feed raw chopped beef instead of the canned meat. Although I have often heard of suggestions that dogs like different foods each day, during my lifelong experience with dogs, and Shelties in particular, I have found that they like continuity in their lives – and food is no exception. The proof of the pudding is in the eating – the key to good animal husbandry is in their health.

WORMING

Your puppy will have been fully wormed when you bought him and while this will give him a good start in life, it will not last forever and a programme consisting of a dosing every three months is a good precaution. In the UK roundworms or tapeworms are really the only ones to dose against. In other countries around the world heartworms are a killer (see Chapter Eleven: Your Sheltie's Health). Wherever you live it is best to be guided by veterinary advice.

VACCINATIONS

You will need to have your puppy vaccinated, and it is generally accepted that this can be done soon after he is eight weeks old, with a second shot given two or four weeks later. Try to take the puppy out on some short fun trips before his visit to the vet so that he is used to travelling in cars.

Puppies need to be vaccinated against distemper, leptospirosis, parvovirus and hepatitis. The modern vaccines are there to protect and the addition of the parvovirus serum to the puppy's vaccination programme has been a blessing.

A certain amount of common sense

has to be used, but as long as the basic vaccination course is completed, your Sheltie should live on into ripe old age.

In countries where rabies in endemic, there is a legal requirement to vaccinate your dog. The first injection is usually given at around six months of age, with boosters every 12 or 36 months.

SOCIALISATION

Although it may seem superfluous, it is very important that your puppy is socialised to meet people and other dogs and to experience the noisy world that us humans have come to think of as normal. Even before the vaccination programme is completed your puppy should be used to riding in the car – there is no need to expose him to risks by taking him out of the safety of the car, he will still be experiencing the hustle and bustle of everyday life. After the vaccination programme is completed your puppy can go out to meet other people and dogs, and once you have accomplished the lead training it might be fun to take him to visit one of the many dog training clubs that are in most towns nowadays. When you

first walk him in the streets, be careful that sudden noises do not frighten him, it is better to build up his confidence slowly.

GROOMING

It is important that you do not over-do the grooming, the whole idea is to socialise your puppy and to get him used to being handled. All our puppies are handled a lot – a daily inspection of tummy, eyes, ears and under the tail, and a weekly trimming of the nails. Once the puppy fluff is sufficiently grown I start putting a little baby talcum powder into the white parts and gently brushing it in using a small, soft brush. So a puppy from a specialist breeder will be used to a small amount of grooming.

With your puppy, you must start as you intend to carry on, and you should get him used to standing on a table. Firstly, put the puppy on the grooming table. Make sure the top is not slippery – a rubber mat can be placed on the table just for this occasion. When you place him on it, tell him to stand, speaking kindly but firmly, and ruffle his coat as encouragement. If he stands still, then tell him what a good boy he is and reward him with a small tidbit. I am a great believer in rewarding good behaviour. On no occasion should you be harsh or rough with your puppy. Shelties are very sensitive and they respond to a gentle voice, a little praise,

Take your puppy out and about as much as possible so that he can experience the sights and sounds of everyday life. This is Mistelin Tanya, owned by Raija Perala in Finland.

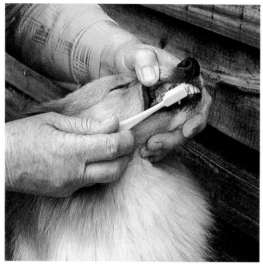

Brush the teeth regularly with a special dog toothpaste. Photo: Haslettt.

Even the back molars need to be cleaned. Photo: Haslettt.

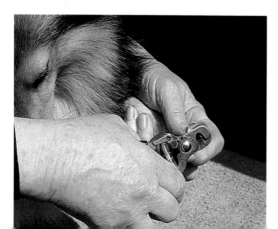

The nails will need regular attention. Photo: Haslettt.

and then a tidbit. If you carry on with this table practise, he will eventually stand good and still; his coat will benefit from the attention, and so will his manners. It can be an irritation to a breeder to have the puppy brought back at a later date with the doting owner saying "he won't stand and let me groom him" – of course he will! He has just learned that you are not the boss after all!

If teeth have a coating of tartar then this should be scraped off with a tooth scraper before brushing. The teeth should stay fairly tartar-free for about the first couple of years.

NAILS

About once a month, perhaps more often if you have field exercise, the nails will need cutting. The first time you do this is a nerve-racking experience. Only the white tip off the end of the nail needs cutting, but when it comes to black nails it is harder to be sure where to cut, so be cautious at first and only cut off a small amount. You can always have a second attempt, but if you cut the nail too short, then it will bleed, and quite profusely too. Do not forget to cut the dewclaw. If this is not done when they are puppies, Shelties can get quite spooked about having their nails clipped. Rather than fight each other, try filing his nails. It takes quite a long time, but could provide a relaxing afternoon for you and your Sheltie!

EARLY TRAINING

I am a great believer in early lead training. It is much less stressful for the puppy to have a collar on at eight weeks than it is for him at six months.

Buy a small, unobtrusive collar and make sure it can fasten fairly tight round the puppy's neck. The lead can be a light nylon one with a safe clip. Even a small puppy can run off should he get free, so be cautious. I like to put the collar on a day before I try the lead. He will scratch at it at first, but ignore all his pleas to remove it. The next day you can clip the lead on, and with a tidbit, call him to come. Be gentle and praise a lot when he does walk. Do not get impatient and pull him along – nothing will be gained, and the trust between you will take a severe set-back if you are too heavy-handed. Coax in a light voice, then praise and reward.

Some puppies will walk on the lead almost straight away, others will take weeks! As the weeks go by, I strongly advise that a check chain is used instead of a collar, but your puppy must be fully lead trained before a check chain is used. Also, change the light training lead to a stronger leather (or nylon) version. In today's traffic a slipped collar or broken lead would be a disaster.

Milesend Stroller: At four months of age, this puppy has already learnt elementary good manners.
Photo: Miles.

5 GROOMING YOUR SHELTIE

One of the pleasures of owning a long-coated breed is keeping the coat nice, and while this can become a problem if neglected, it should be one of those maintenance jobs that, if done frequently, is easily managed.

GROOMING THE PET DOG

Puppy grooming is as much training as proper grooming, but once past the six month stage, the coat starts to grow at quite a rate, and this can be encouraged with a little know-how. For serious grooming I advise getting a frame to fasten on the table, as this makes life a lot easier. These frames can be purchased at a big show or via mail order, and will fix easily onto most table tops. However, these are not a necessity, and grooming can be done by placing the dog on a firm table – make sure it does not have a slippery surface, as this will destroy the dog's confidence. Make him stand still, and praise and reward if he does so. You must be firm, not rough or impatient, but when you say "Stand", your dog should not question the command – after all, he knows that a bit of praise and a tidbit will be his reward!

For everyday grooming I check all over for anything unpleasant – see that the corners of the eyes are free from matter, that his ears are not dirty and that there is no dirt under his tail. This should not happen if the dog is fed on a consistent diet. I am often surprised at the number of people who tell me that their Shelties have dirty trousers. Mine do not! Then give the coat a little spritz with either plain water, or any mild made-up lotion in a fine spray bottle; I sometimes add a little antiseptic to the water, or if you want him to smell nice try adding a little perfume. Rub this in well using your hands. Take one of the bristle brushes and start a gentle yet rigorous brush, starting with the rear of the dog, so that all of his coat, including

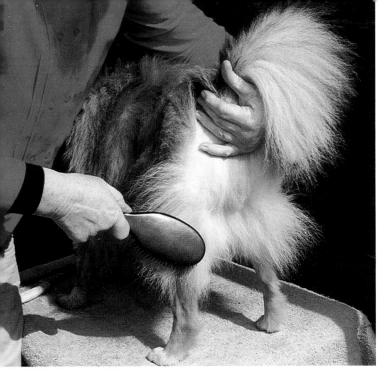

Start grooming at the rear.

the tail, gets a thorough grooming down to the skin. Make sure that you go under the tummy line and inside the legs. Take great care to brush the bib up well, and also behind the ears, where those soft hairs can tangle. This is a good toning-up for the dog, and he should thoroughly enjoy it – if he does not, perhaps you are a bit rough or grumbling at him instead of praising!

Once I have him looking like a hedgehog, I put the dog to the floor

with much praise and a little tidbit. He will always shake his coat back into some sort of shape, and then up on the table again. If he is casting, it is necessary to constantly empty the brush of hair. This second brushing is the toning and shaping. Brush the coat in layers – I always start at the rear and groom a layer down in its natural fall, then to the next layer, so that eventually the whole of the dog has been given a second 'going-over'.

Brush the coat in layers right down to the skin.

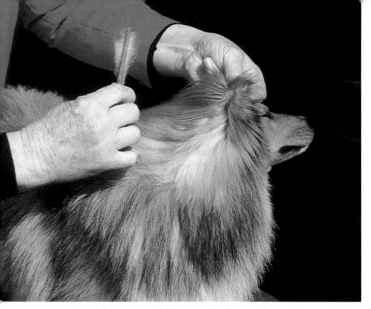

Take special care to comb out the softer ear featherings.
Photos: Haslett.

With your wide-toothed comb you should just tease out the trousers and the bib. With the finer comb, you can comb his face, behind the ears, forelegs and hind legs below the hock. If one of my Shelties is in a very heavy moult, I will dispense with the brush altogether and, using the wide-toothed comb, I will comb it out in layers, starting at the rear end as before. A bitch which has reared a litter, or a youngster at about a year old, can shed coat at an alarming rate – it is almost useless to brush if the dog has got to this stage, as the brush will need emptying with every stroke.

The wide-toothed comb will rake out bundles of dead hair. Do not be alarmed, it will grow back again, and all the quicker for this attention.

ANAL GLANDS
It is a sensible precaution to occasionally empty your Sheltie's anal glands. It may well save a trip to the vet at a later date, and, though unpleasant, it is all part of keeping your dog in good order. Stand him on the table, lift his tail and feel either side of the rectum. With a good swab of cotton wool, using your thumb and forefinger liberally covered with the swab, squeeze and gently pull forward and very slightly upwards. It does not hurt the dog, but it might give you an unpleasant surprise if the squirt of foul-smelling fluid misses the swab!

BATHING
It is essential to bath your dog from time to time. There is no excuse for having a dirty dog. I do like to bath the puppies, as this not only cleans them, but teaches them that, although strange, a bath is enjoyable, and there is a lot of praise and that special tidbit afterwards.

There are many different shampoos on the market. The ones especially made for dogs really are much better than the ones made for human hair, and it is not sensible to use washing-up liquid – these are made to reduce grease, and you do not want to dry out their skins. Select the shampoo that suits your dog's coat best. I always

Assemble your grooming kit before you start bathing.

shampoo is well worked-in all over the body, and up each leg. The dirt will lift off with the first rinse, and to get that extra gleaming whiteness I will often go over the whole process again.

Try to be quick, as you have only accomplished the easy bit so far! Once the second rinse has been thoroughly done, put a big warm towel around the dog and pat dry. Rub the forelegs, face and hind legs (below the hock) until dry, and then put your dog down – preferably outside, as they always have a lovely shake, with water droplets going everywhere. It usually stirs up a bit of excitement and the dog that has been bathed will feel on top of the world!

Do not let the body hair dry naturally as it will dry like a blanket, and you will have a fearsome job combing it all out once dry. After allowing that shake, which will have got rid of quite a lot of moisture, put your dog up on a table, and, armed with the hairdryer in one hand and your Mason Pearson brush in the other, you have the long job of drying. Start with the face – not too close, as no-one likes warm air blowing in their eyes, then progress in layers, taking care to dry the hair at the back of the ears. Work down the dog, brushing and drying all the way down the bib and along the body. Try to separate a layer and dry it thoroughly before moving on to the next section. Just to dry the top would leave that dense undercoat still damp, so make sure to dry right down to the skin. Once you

dilute shampoo by pouring a small quantity into a plastic mug, and then adding hot water. This means that the mixture is warm and the dog is not subjected to a sudden coldness on their skin, and that it is much easier to rinse off when the shampoo is not applied too thickly. If you have a shower then the end result is much better than rinsing the dog off in his own bath water.

I stand my dog in the bath, check that the water through the shower is warm and not too hot. Wet the dog thoroughly all over, including the face and tummy, and being careful to include behind the ears and under the tail. Once wetted thoroughly, apply the shampoo mixture all over the dog. The head can have a cursory clean, as the hair is smooth, but make sure that the

35

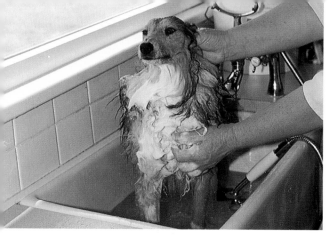

After damping the coat, apply the shampoo and work into a rich lather.

Spray the coat lightly and brush in sections. make sure you groom down to the skin.

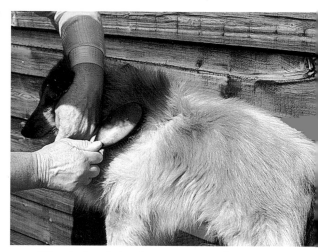

Make sure all the shampoo is rinsed off.

Use the brush in vigorous yet gentle strokes.

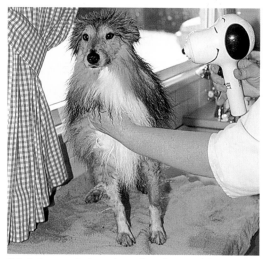
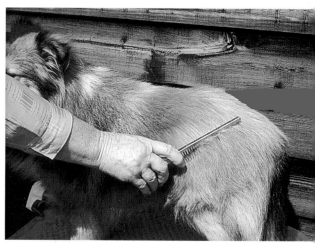

Lightly towel-dry, then dry thoroughly with a hair-dryer.

Once the coat is brushed all over, use the wide-toothed comb to shape.

have completed this, shape the coat down with the wide-toothed comb, and look at any of those long straggly hairs that would look better trimmed off.

GROOMING THE SHOW DOG

It has often been said that 'show' people manage to portray much more profusion of coat on their dogs than the average 'pet' owner, and although coats vary a lot in their density and length, I think the answer is in the coat care.

To groom the dog as a matter of routine, it is always best to start by dampening the coat, this will give it more body and prevent it from lying flat. Even after bathing prior to a show I still 'spritz' the coat and rub in well before starting to brush. Do not forget to brush in sections; I always start at he rear of the dog, so in fact the hair above the hocks is my first section, working

up the thigh, then the tail, then progressing from rear to head along the dog. Just to brush the topcoat would leave the undercoat ungroomed and your dog would get that 'clumpy' look, whereas if you brush right to the skin, your Sheltie will end up with every hair separated and the coat will have lift and body. While for home grooming you can use talcum powder and coat dressings, in the UK it is not permitted for any additives to be used on, or in, the coat when preparing for the show ring.

We like to think of our breed as natural, and apart from the bathing, spritzing and grooming, the only other show preparation is trimming of the ears and feet, and tooth cleaning, which are all essential. In the US, dogs are presented very differently; much more trimmed, chalked white and with coats

TRIMMING
Photos: Haslett.

Cut the untidy hair between the toes. This is done by pulling the hair up between the toes and cutting level with the foot.

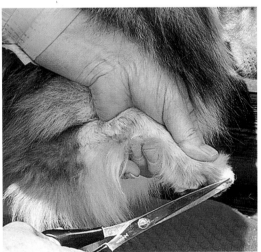

Shape the foot into an oval shape.

much more 'stand-off'. Professional groomers and handlers are often used.

TRIMMING

FEET: Obviously, the feet need trimming. The foot should be oval in shape, and the appearance can be helped by trimming with sharp scissors on the side and back, and not so close on the front two toes. Soft fluffy bits of hair, often quite straggly, grow in between all four toes, and should be lifted up then trimmed along the line of the foot. Do not take the scissors between the toes, as you might end up with the foot looking star-shaped.

EARS: The ears will almost certainly need a little trimming, but retaining a little feathering and not too severe, or that gentle expression will soon be lost. Using finger and thumb, pluck any obvious straggly bits, then comb again to see what else needs to come off. Fold the ear in half and look carefully at the ears lifted into the 'show' position. Be careful with the scissoring, as it will ruin all your work to be too heavy-handed. Just trim off the excess around the tip – not too close, or the ear will look harsh and terrier-like, then perhaps a final finger-and-thumb plucking round the back and base of the ear. With the ears looking tidy, but still feathered, the whole look of soft appeal can be achieved. If in doubt, it is much better to leave hair on than to remove it.

HOCKS: Below the hock is another area where hair must be removed, as Shelties grow rather straggly hair here. Comb this through upwards and outwards with your fine-toothed comb, and make an assessment of where to cut

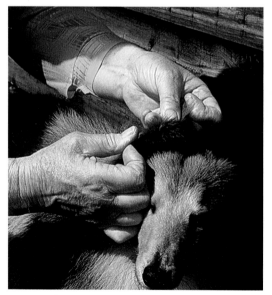

Use the finger and thumb method to remove the long straggly hairs behind the ears.

Tidy the ears into shape with the thinning scissors.

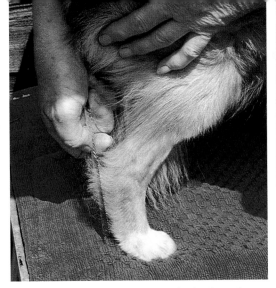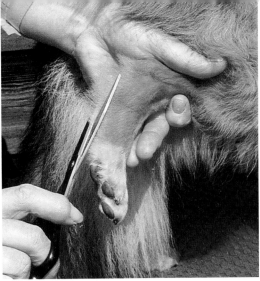

Comb the hair out below the hock and cut in a straight line.

Be careful not to cut the hair too close.

– in a straight line, not too close to the bone. I find it much easier to cut upwards, from the back of the foot up to the hock. If in doubt, cut longer rather than shorter – you can always have a second try. The dog will look to have poor bone if you cut too close, and Shelties are meant to have well-rounded bone. Your dog will be ready for the show ring after this, and all you may need to do is to clean his teeth.

If your Sheltie is purely a pet and not a show dog, I still hope that you will follow a grooming programme through pride of ownership as well as for the benefit of the dog. Trimming is not essential in a pet dog, but all dogs, like people, improve with a little beautifying! Those long straggly hairs that grow between the toes can be combed up and cut off; the foot can be tidied by trimming around the oval shape of the foot. The ears should always be kept free of any tangles, but can probably still be improved by

trimming off that excessive straggly hair. It goes without saying that the pet dog should have his nails and teeth done just like the show dog.

PROBLEM EARS
Even though you have purchased your puppy from the best kennel and he has a pedigree dotted with Champions, there can be no guarantee that his ears will stay in the natural semi-erect position. It is strange that both parents can have perfectly natural ears, and yet their offspring might well have ear problems. Usually, the cause is through cutting those adult teeth, so from about 14 weeks onwards be vigilant, and if either of your puppy's ears 'fly' up, then you must get the ear over or the muscles will strengthen in the 'up' position. For just a little care at this stage, you can prevent the ears being pricked for the rest of the puppy's life. By far the easiest method is to chew some chewing gum until soft and pliable, then, pulling off a

Ch. Sandpiper Of Sharval (Ch. Sharval The Delinquent – Charnwood Gay Girl), owned by Albert Wight. The first Sheltie to win BIS at an All Breeds Championship Show, groomed to perfection.
Photo: Diane Pearce.

bit with wetted fingers, stick it firmly on the inside tip of the ears. If you put on too much the ear will droop over too much, if not enough the ear will stay pricked, so it is a question of trial and error. I would suggest that if you stick a small bit on, you can always add to it.

Once stuck in place, the gum will stay on for a month or so. After it has fallen off, you might well have to renew the weight, as the ears will probably take several months to settle.

However, if the puppy's ear falls to a droop position, you will need to cut a small piece of chiropodists' plaster and cover the crease, pressing firmly. Lift the ear into the semi-erect position; if there is a lot of heavy fluff, it is well worth while cutting this off, as not only will the ear benefit from losing the weight of the hair, it will also allow the air to circulate, which, in turn, will benefit the natural fold. This 'brace' will need to stay in the ear for several weeks, and should it work loose, replace before the ear flops again. If you are showing your Sheltie and his ears continue to be troublesome, then you must not weight them with chewing gum as it will be very difficult to remove, and you do not want the embarrassment of a mark being seen on the ear by the judge. Better under these circumstances to use a sticking plaster (zinc oxide plaster is ideal), as this will weight the ear beautifully but can be easily removed for that all-important show.

If the ears have dropped to what I term the 'frying pan' position, then you will need to trim off excess hair and make a brace with chiropodist's tape across the top of the head, joining one ear to the other. This looks unsightly and is easily knocked out of place if you have more than one dog, so if you have the stamina to segregate the puppy for a while this method does work!

Sometimes the ears are still very supple, and you may be lucky enough to be able to soften the half-way crease with hand cream or baby oil, and just massage the ear in half. This helps a great deal, and the puppy often enjoys the attention. At no time should the dog feel pain or discomfort. If you have used oil of any sort and then later decide to use plaster or chewing gum as a weight, you must wash and dry the ear leather thoroughly, or nothing will adhere to it. It does seem a bit like cheating, but hopefully it will only be a phase, and is well worth your perseverance. When breeding Shelties it is always best to go for natural ears in both parents.

6 *TRAINING YOUR SHELTIE*

One of the very nice things about the Sheltie is its versatility. If you wanted to show your Sheltie but he has not come up to standard, there are many other activities you can enjoy. One of the most popular is Obedience training, and this is one of the most rewarding and absorbing of hobbies. Shelties are very intelligent and very quick to learn. Competition Obedience is great fun and there have been several Obedience Champions in our breed. If you intend to show, you will have to train your Sheltie for the show ring, and I really would not recommend proceeding with Obedience training – you can teach the dog to stand instead of sit, but you run a risk of doing neither well. It would be a lovely thought that someone might make a dual Champion, but it has not been achieved yet.

OBEDIENCE TRAINING
Most Obedience training clubs will not accept a puppy for training until he is six months old, but there is so much you can do at home. Once the vaccinations are over, you must socialise your puppy so that he is perfectly accustomed to other dogs, children and general hubbub. Nothing is more off-putting to both your puppy and to other people than you shouting or jerking heavily on the check chain. Shelties are sensitive and they know your mood almost before you do! Start as you mean to go on, and once the initial lead training is accomplished, you can start encouraging that lovely close heel work. It will only work as long as you and your puppy are in harmony.

THE BASICS
To begin, the only equipment you will need is a thin check chain and a light leather lead. Make sure that the chain collar is long enough to easily go over the head and to leave you a few inches from the neck to the clip of the lead. On

no account have the check chain so long that it forms part of the lead, and also, once the lead is unleashed, you do not want a long piece of chain dangling down as this will be very distracting to the dog.

It is very important that you do not over-train your puppy, expecting too much, too soon. It is much better to limit your training sessions to 10 to 15 minutes each day, using this time together to build up a relationship. I am a great believer in the reward system of training. If the puppy knows that a small tidbit will follow if he does something he is told to do, then he will sparkle and show anticipation. One of the worst things to combat is boredom. Personally, I hate to hear shouting. My Shelties respond to a 'cooing' command, then praise in the form of an intimate "clever boy".

Although it is better to train away from distractions, of course your Sheltie will have to perform these exercises in different environments. You may receive one or two enquiring glances but it might be a good idea to have a quiet practise next time you and he go shopping in town.

Rome was not built in a day – nor will Obedience training be accomplished in a day! It is absolutely pointless to train if you are in an 'off' mood; better to skip a day than to lose patience. Try not to keep talking to him – it is better to give the command in a clear, concise voice, then be effusive in your praise when he has achieved the exercise.

HEEL WORK

Encourage close heel work right from the start. Your dog will always be expected to work on your left side, so be sure that the check chain is on easy release on his right side. The chain will be a reminder to him – it can be jerked taut and instantly slackened if he is not paying attention, or not trotting close enough to you. It is important to encourage this close heel work – it is the basis of all Obedience exercises. Ideally, the dog's head should be just forward of

Attentive Heelwork: Kyloe Piper (The Meadsman At Myriehewe – Seavall Becky At Kyloe). Bred by Mrs J. Hardman, owned by Mrs A. Smith.

your left knee. Find out his normal pace and adjust yours accordingly; you will be expected to be able to accomplish fast and slow pace, but that is in the future. Start off with lots of encouragement – "Heel – good boy", or, if he bounds ahead, then exert a quick jerk/release action on his chain with commands of "Heel" until he deserves your praise. On no account allow him to pull on the lead – this must be checked from the beginning with lots of jerk/release actions, followed by praise. If he is pulling to get ahead, be sure that your pace is fast enough. Try to develop crisp foot work; it must be very muddling for him to follow clumsy feet. Make sure that he is happy, alert and keen on his heel work before you move on to the second exercise, which is the Sit.

SIT

This is easy to teach, and, being relatively small dogs, Shelties find it easy to sit and look up at you. Start the exercise by finishing your heel work, then jerk/release the chain and press gently on his hindquarters with the command "Sit" (make sure that your diction is precise and do not forget to sound the 'T'). He will usually sit at this command, so follow immediately by praise and a tidbit. Walk forward a few paces, stop and command again. Without allowing the lesson to become boring, try this several times, making sure that he sits quickly, as this is all-

important in competition Obedience. It will not take long for you to perfect this exercise.

One word of warning. When you first initiate the sit command, make sure that you press on the dog's hindquarters, or even the root of the tail, but do not press on the centre of the dog's back.

STAY

Having mastered the sit exercise, it is time to proceed on to the stay command. The best way to accomplish this is to intersperse your heel work

Build up the Stay exercise in stages. Photo: Haslett.

with some sit commands, making sure he is paying attention, and with the flat of your hand showing to his face say, gently but firmly, "Stay". With your right leg, quietly walk a pace or two forward to the end of the lead, repeating "Stay" in a low drawn-out voice.

It will in all probability take a few exercises for him to understand that you want him to stay put – once you are confident that he will stay, go to the end of the lead and walk around him, joining him as if it was the sit exercise, then praise him. Practise this until you are sure that he knows the meaning of the word stay. You will be able to progress to walking up to him, and, without breaking your stride, making sure that your left leg leads off once you are parallel with him, add the command "Heel", and off you both should go.

You and he have perfected three important things - heel on a lead, sit, and stay. Have you enjoyed the training – and even more importantly, has he? There is no use in progressing if you are not enjoying the challenge. Remember, even in top competition, it must be fun – he will lag and look bored if his interest is not stimulated all of the time. If you feel confident enough to start another exercise, the next one to try is the down.

DOWN

The down always seems a lot harder than the sit, which seems a more natural position. Start off with your usual heel work practise, a few sits and a stay. Finish on a good note with lots of praise and a tidbit. Now is the time to try the down.

While he is in the sit position, drop your voice and tell him, in a clear voice, to go "down". Jerk/release the lead to the floor, and press gently but firmly on the shoulders. Make it a rapid process, and then praise. Try this several times; it will take quite a few lessons to get an unaided response. Do not be tempted to shout your command, better to jerk/release.

When playing in the house, it might be beneficial to sit him, facing you, and place a tidbit a few yards in front of him. Say one precise word – "down" – and he is not far from his tidbit. Push it to him with 'cooing' praise – what a clever boy! Hopefully he will be anxious to please you, and will soon understand that he is rewarded when he downs on command.

The tone of your voice should be quite different – sit is higher pitched, with definite emphasis on the 'T'. When giving the command down, try to drop your voice and emphasise the 'ow' part of the word. Shelties are quick to learn, and once he knows the difference between the two words, his response should be rapid.

If you are practising your heel work and you feel confident enough, try dropping him into the down position, and follow with the stay command. If this is successful, walk on, trying to gauge your footwork so that your right leg leads away. If he does not instantly drop on the down command, do not walk on. You must get this exercise right before progressing.

You can start leaving him in both the sit and down stay positions, unclipping his lead and walking off. Make this a short trip at first, and as his confidence grows make your absence longer, and progress to even going out of sight. If he should break the stay command, begin all over again. Remember that your own quiet home is quite a different environment to the Obedience ring, where the distractions will be many. When you are doing this exercise at an Obedience training club, try to find a space in the line-up away from some of the breeds that might frighten him. He will become rock steady eventually, but there is no need to tempt providence and risk putting him off before you have given it a chance.

OFF THE LEAD
All the while we have been talking about training I have said how invaluable the jerk/release method is of correcting your Sheltie, or of stimulating interest. If you are confident, try heel work off the lead – should any adjustment be needed, do not use your voice except in encouragement, but bend down and jerk the end of his chain collar, just as if he were on a lead. That jerk/release

movement is a reminder; free he may be, but he is still on parade!

If he is wandering, not paying attention, or constantly staring at the other dogs, then he is not ready for heel off-lead, so go back to lead work and use the jerk/release method until he is close and responsive. It might be a good idea to add curves and circles to your heel work to stimulate interest. I am a great believer in bribery — do not be afraid to use that tidbit to get his response.

When you are out for everyday exercise, your Sheltie will be used to coming when you call him. Try not to shout, but use a high, urgent voice calling his name in two syllables. Always reward.

RECALL
The recall is different as you are calling your dog in to you from sit or down position, and you want instant response, with him running straight towards you, almost nosing into your thighs, and sitting straight in front of you. This is unbelievably easy to teach as long as you reward.

Try a short distance at first. Stand facing him, having given him the instruction to sit, stay, then walk off with your right foot leading, and stop a few paces ahead of him. Turn to face him, place your legs slightly apart and straighten up, open out your arms, while at the same time calling his name in a light but firm voice. As he runs towards you, bring your two hands into your crotch, encouraging him to run in close to sniff at your hands, hoping for a reward, then in a quiet voice, command sit. If he wanders, or delays, then encourage with your voice and a tidbit.

Just think of all you have achieved – heel work on-lead, sit, stay, down, heel work off-lead and recall. Now it is time to teach the finish, and this is harder than you would think.

THE FINISH

At all times, your dog will be expected to end the exercise with a clean and tidy finish. This is where he automatically returns to your left side, sits straight and looks up at you, hoping for that word of praise.

There are two ways of achieving the finish. One is to encourage the dog round your right side, behind, and then to sit neatly on your left. The other is to encourage him to your left, and to turn on his own axis to a sit. You must decide which method you find easier.

Both methods start with your dog sitting facing you (as in the recall). For the former, say in a light but firm voice "heel", and, with pressure on the lead from your right hand, encourage him quickly round you to a straight sit beside you. Praise and reward. Always make sure that he is sitting straight. In competition, he will lose valuable points if you allow him to get in the habit of a crooked sit.

For the second method of teaching the finish, this time you put pressure on the lead with your left hand as you say "heel", once again making sure that he ends in a straight sit. Praise and reward.

It is important to get the finish right. All exercises end with the dog sitting at your left side, so it is worth a lot of practise to perfect this to look slick and professional.

Try to finish on a praiseworthy note, and always end up with him in the Sit position beside you. Then, in a different tone of voice, use your own words as a finish – "off you go" is my favourite phrase, then a little play, and the bond is welding stronger and stronger between you.

COMPETING

Some of the Sheltie clubs run Obedience classes in conjunction with their shows, and if you have trained your Sheltie to the standard so far described, why not give him an outing? Can your nerves stand it? The Sheltie club in your area may not be able to incorporate Obedience, in which case you will have to make your debut at an all-breeds Obedience show. You will now know how important it has been to socialise your dog to other breeds. Do not try to be over-ambitious, enter the class with the minimum requirements!

ADVANCED TRAINING

It is a lovely thought when you have

The intelligent Sheltie can compete in advanced obedience. Photo: Hardman.

Kyloe Piper presents the dumbell to his handler. Photo: Hardman.

won some pre-beginners or beginners classes. There is always more to achieve.

RETRIEVING

Most dogs love playing, and puppies often show their aptitude for retrieving at an early age. I am convinced that some strains are better retrievers than others – it can be easy to teach, or it can be very difficult. Hoping that you find it easy, the best way to teach the retrieve is as an extension of playing. Throw a toy and request its return, much the

same as you would for recall. Use the word "hold" until you are ready to take the toy, then finish. It is so easy and so much fun! Pity the poor owner who has got on well with their training programme, only to find that their biddable little Sheltie just will not retrieve, and sometimes will not even hold an article in his mouth. You should show absolutely no anger, only encouragement.

A sure way of encouraging him to take something in his mouth is to rub a

Scent discrimination is no problem to Kyloe Piper.   *Photo: Hardman.*

piece of cooked liver on the article, opening his mouth and popping the retrieve article in his mouth, saying "hold" and cooing your praise at him. Once he has found that the retrieve object is not so foreign, then you have more chance of him eventually learning to pick it up for himself. It might take a while and lots of patience from you.

ADVANCED RECALL

You will need to teach advanced recall, where your dog has to come to heel while you are walking. It is a pleasant exercise to learn and most Shelties are brilliant at it.

The heel work off-lead has been perfected, and you are confident that, once your Sheltie is in the sit-stay

position, you can continue walking off, turning to right and left, then an about-turn. Watch him out of the corner of your eye. Has he stayed, and is he alertly watching you? Call his name in a crisp, clear voice and keep moving at a slick pace, then say "heel" as he approaches. Keep him at heel for a while, then start the procedure all over again. Do not go on too long as boredom will set in.

As you progress with his training, there are lots of different exercises to teach him – stand, scent, distant control and the send away are all advanced exercises for him to master. It would not be beneficial to try too many new ventures – better by far to perfect the first training exercises, and always remember that it is meant to be fun for both of you.

AGILITY

If you do not fancy the discipline of Obedience, why not consider Agility? It is such fun for dogs and owners. You cannot start training your Sheltie for Agility as a puppy as, quite sensibly, it is thought better for bones to develop before the stress of jumps and weaving etc, so you should wait until your Sheltie is over a year old. Agility classes are graded for the height of the dog – 'Mini' is for dogs of 15 ins and under, with the jumps up to 15 ins high. 'Midi' is for dogs of 15 to 17 ins, who are expected to jump up to 2 ft 6 ins. The 'Senior' size is, obviously, for dogs of

Agility provides excellent exercise for dog and hander, as well as being mentally stimulating. Hanburyhill Blue Heather at Valdug (Ch. Cultured At Cashella – Marklin Estella). Bred by Rev & Mrs Hambrey, owned by Mrs V. Johnson. Photo: Rouillard.

over 17 ins, and they are expected to clear jumps the same as Border Collies or Retrievers etc. With a breed like ours that does vary in size, it is possible to find Shelties represented in all three grades!

It is necessary to teach a certain amount of discipline as your dog will have to sit to start off. He will have to down and stay on the table. Other than these few rules, the whole exercise is

achieved with the excited animation of your Sheltie enjoying himself on the course. As you are expected to run with the dog, it is beneficial exercise for you too.

Clearing the hurdles: Fernslope Blu-U-No At Valdug (Pepperhill Gifted N'Black – Fernslope True Blue). Bred by Mrs R. Davenport, owned by Mrs V. Johnson. Photo: R. Mitchell.

Agility has a big following in the US.   *Photo courtesy: Rebecca Golatzki.*

Through the tyre: Fernslope Blu-U-No At Valdug.   *Photo: R. Mitchell.*

Fourwinds Face The Nation in winnng form. Photo courtesy: Rebecca Golatzki.

JUMPING

To begin training him over jumps, it is better if you jump with him. Start with the smallest of jumps; a broom handle straddling two bricks would be ideal. Place him in the sit position beside you, and when ready, give your command to jump, as you run forward with the dog running along excitedly at your side. Once you have both cleared the jump, give him much praise.

An alternative method of getting him to jump is to throw something over the obstacle – a favourite toy, his ball or even some bait. You can continue throwing the toy as an incentive to tackle several hurdles.

With him now enjoying his first lessons, it will not be long before you can point at the jump, and animatedly tell him to "go jump". He will soon realise that this is what you are going to reward him for.

He will need to jump through a tyre, and here again, start off with this just resting upright on the ground. Give lots of praise when you get him to jump through it, then as confidence grows, so this too can be raised.

WEAVING

Weaving poles can pose a problem to teach – your dog will have to know heel and away. Approach the weaving poles as you would any new exercise – take it slowly at first. You will be surprised just how quickly he learns to weave in and out of the poles, following your

Negotiating the weaving poles: Yaldug Shelley Is Blue (Ch. Swiftlight Othello – Fernslope Blu-U-No at Valdug). Bred by Mrs Johnson, owned by Sarah Barette. Photo: David Ferguson.

Small and agile, weaving can be made to look easy.
Photo courtesy: Rebecca Golatzki.

alternate commands to heel and away.

You might find it helpful if the poles are placed a further distance apart at first, then gradually decrease the space between each pole to the regulation.

THE TUNNEL

Learning to go through the tunnel can be arduous – you may have to squeeze through yourself along with the dog. Alternatively, ask a friend to assist by holding your dog at one end of the tunnel, while you call his name from the other. If he is reluctant, perhaps try a shorter distance in case he loses confidence half way through the tunnel. Once through, praise and reward. Always end on a good note. If you feel patience ebbing, then wait for another day!

OTHER ACTIVITIES

You could try Working Trials, where you will still need an element of Obedience training, but the precision is less, and your dog will learn to use his brain.

There are some people interested in Herding. Shelties often have a natural aptitude for rounding things up, and to teach herding is an extension of this.

There is Flyball, where a ball is released from a spring trap by the dog himself by treading on a pedal, then allowing him to catch the ball in mid air. It is marvellous to watch and the agile build of the Sheltie makes him a natural for this sporty game.

There is also Heel work to Music. The first demonstration I saw of this

Duffy, owned by Daniel Jet, emerges from the tunnel.
Photo courtesy: Rebecca Golatzki.

Dual Champions in Canada: OT Ch. & Ch. Sunara Drift On Misty Glen, owned by Jo Rayner, with his son OT Ch. Am. Can. Ch. Seachant Indigo Mystery CDX, owned by Leslie Leggett.
Photo: Dallas Sissons.

was wonderful. The Shelties seemed to be as one with their owner and they really enjoyed themselves. On reflection, I was left with a feeling that perhaps my physique would not complement the dog's!

If you are interested in any of these activities, the best thing would be to get in touch with your breed club. Even if they do not hold the training, they will most probably know who does.

USA COMPETITIONS
The American Kennel Club has offered Obedience and Tracking competitions (at first combined) since the 1930s. More recently, AKC Herding was introduced in the 1980s, and AKC Agility was added in 1995. AKC titles based on passing scores, not on competition, are:

OBEDIENCE: CD (Companion dog) – basic flat work, on and off lead; CDX (Companion dog excellent) – add retrieves, jumping, out of sight stays; UD (Utility dog) – hand signals, directed retrieves, directed jumping, scent discrimination; UDX (Utility dog excellent) – 10 same-day qualifying scores in Utility and Open.

TRACKING: TD (Tracking dog) – quarter mile track, half hour to 2 hours old; TDX (Tracking dog excellent) – half mile track with cross tracks, obstacles, 3 to 5 hours old, multiple article drops; VST (Variable surface tracking) – mixes vegetated and non-vegetated terrain.

HERDING: HT (Herding tested) – basic control around livestock, small arena; PT (Pre-trial tested) – larger arena, handler can still move with dog but dog must control livestock; HS (herding started) – dog must lift stock and drive while handler stays at post;

The Sheltie can compete on equal terms in all Obedience disciplines.

Am. Ch. Manabrook's Dusty Wrangler CD, TD, owned by Mary Mahaffey, shows off his tracking skills.

Photos courtesy: Mary Mahaffey.

Ch. Lambur Good Times Murph UDT. Only the seventh Ch UDT Sheltie in the US. Bred by Wade S. Burns and Jon Woodring, owned by Mary Mahaffey. Photo courtesy: Mary Mahaffey.

HI (Herding intermediate) – more restrictions on handler; HX (Herding advanced) – handler must stay stationary except during penning.

AGILITY: NA (Novice agility) – simple course, no weaves; OA (Open agility) – more advanced course, weaves; AX (Agility excellent) – complex courses, weaves; MX (master agility) – ten legs past AX.

In addition to the titles above, which are based on meeting minimum qualifying scores, performance Championships (competitive) are possible. The obedience trial championship (OTCH) is awarded when a dog accumulates 100 points after the UD. Points are won by taking first or second place in Utility or Open classes. The Herding Championship is also earned by accumulating points in competition in the advanced class. A dog who passes all three tracking tests is designated a Champion Tracker. An agility championship is currently in the discussion stage. Herding competition is basically within the herding group; other performance events are normally open to all breeds (unless held at a breed Specialty).

SHOW TRAINING

Often I have heard people say that they would like to start showing their Sheltie. Once your Sheltie is a little older, depressing as it may seem, I would think this almost impossible. As Shelties are shown on a loose lead, they have to be schooled from the start. With one of the many breeds that can be placed and then held on a tight lead, known as 'stacking', it may well be possible to adapt to the show ring, but a Sheltie is expected to stand and 'show' his ears, on a long, loose lead, and this is a lot harder than it looks. Training must be started early.

As soon as you have decided which puppy is the show prospect, lesson one must be to get him happy and used to standing on a table, and this is covered in Chapter Four. Now you must start giving him a tidbit to get him interested in lifting his ears, and you must find five minutes every day to put the puppy on the table and coax that animated

Herding Tests are strongly supported in the US, and the Shetland Sheepdog has shown willingness and apptitude.
Photos courtesy: Rebecca Golatzki.

57

Jasper, pictured after winning his first puppy match, shows the animation needed in a show dog. Photo: Haslett.

Ch. Francehill Andy Pandy (Ch. Francehill Persimon – Francehill Frangipani) responding to his young handler, April Searle.

attention. Give him lots of praise when you get him to stay still and look at the tidbit. I cannot emphasise enough that show training must be made a pleasure; if you chastise and keep correcting the puppy, he will lose that sparkle and will start showing with reluctance.

Most people vaccinate their puppies before they are three months old, and after this age it is advisable to start going to a training class. Most areas have a dog club, and these clubs often run a ring training class. These are not only beneficial to the puppy, but they can be fun and quite socialising for their owners too! If you do your homework and your puppy is well-schooled, you can look forward to the start of his show career with confidence.

While ringcraft classes are invaluable for getting the puppy used to other breeds and for general socialisation, the most important part of all training is

All attention in the show ring: Ch. Miss Mandy Of Dunbrae At Faradale (Cinnamon Cascade Of Diomed – Myriehewe Scarlet O'Hara). Bred by Ian Shovelton, owned by Mr and Mrs Jackson.

done at home. It is up to you to give confidence to the puppy. Make sure that as soon as the show lead goes on, he knows that you expect show behaviour. You must feel assured that he will look at your hand or pocket as soon as you stand in show pose – I usually make a special little noise that indicates that I will give a tidbit if I get that animated attention. All this response is drilled into the puppy at home.

Movement and construction are very important in the Sheltie, so you must train the puppy to show off his

Ch. Edglonian Rocking Robin: A perfect example of the loose lead technique demonstrated by Debbie Pearson. Photo: Roy Pearson.

movement to the best advantage. He will have learnt to trot on the lead beside you, neither pulling ahead nor lagging behind. In Obedience training, you need to teach the puppy to move really close beside you, but for show training you want a good distance between you both, so start as you mean to continue. The way to keep a distance between you is to stop, command that he stays, and then you move a step away. Watching the Shelties moving around the ring is often the judge's way of ascertaining outline, tail carriage and the true effortless movement that we are all striving for. The individual moving up and down the ring – or in a triangle – is to view the soundness. Make sure that when you are asked to move, you have that distance between you and the puppy.

PHOTOGRAPHING YOUR SHELTIE

I cannot help but suppress a smile – I can imagine my friends' and family's reaction to this title! However, being next to useless at photography myself does not stop me from telling others how it should be done!

If you want a snapshot of your Sheltie puppy to send back to his breeder to let them know how he is progressing, then life is easy. All you need is a lovely background, infinite patience and a full roll of film. Eventually your puppy will move into an appropriate position and you will be able to take several snaps of

the same subject, on the assumption that at least one will come out well. Personally, I love all photos that are sent to me at Christmas time and take great pleasure in displaying them all.

If you want to photograph that up-and-coming show specimen, then this is a different matter, and it is essential that the dog appears at his best. Obviously the dog should be presented to the camera in the same condition that he would be shown to a judge, so keep your brush with you in case some readjustment is needed.

I have mentioned the importance of show training, and hopefully your dog will know to stand on command. Once you are satisfied that all his legs are in the right place, move as far from the dog as is possible. It is very annoying if the Sheltie creeps forward, but keep patient as the end result will be worth it. Your Sheltie will have learned to stand and show for the tidbit in your hand; keep those ears in an alert position up on the head, and if he flags, toss a piece of food a little distance ahead of him. This usually stretches the neck, so you get that lovely outline of the head held high. Although I am advocating tossing something on the ground to attract that extra alert look, please do not be tempted to do this in the show ring.

If you are taking outdoor photographs, you will need to check the position of the sun – there is no point in ruining the picture with the

*Ch. Shelto Sheraleigh:
Symmetrical pose at home.
Photo: Moore.*

*Ch. Miss
Mandy Of
Dunbrae At
Faradale: A
beautiful,
natural
photograph
taken in the
Pendle Hills.
Photo: Jackson.*

Ch. Cultured At Cashella (tricolour) and Ch. Mountmoor Blue Boy (blue merle): Black and white photography can be stunning.

photographer's shadow in view – and also check the wind direction. Even those perfect, natural ears can look less than perfect if the wind catches them, and it would be annoying if the best photograph made your Sheltie appear 'prick-eared', or with his beautifully groomed coat blown out of position. The background will need to be uncluttered – short grass gives a lovely colour and uninterrupted vision of the dog himself, and somehow Shelties look at their best on grass. It is not advisable to stand the dog on a table to be photographed, as it is virtually impossible to get that alert attention. Avoid the temptation to point the camera down on the dog. It is much

Winster Whatnot, bred and owned by Mr and Mrs J.C. Randall. You need a mixture of good luck and quick timing to take this type of photo.   *Photo: Randall.*

better to be on the same level as the subject being photographed, and this often means the photographer being prostrate on the ground, while the dog is walked into position. A kneeling or crouching position will be necessary, at least.

I think it is recognised among Sheltie folk that a side-on photograph is best – you can see the outline of the dog, and the construction, neck and head profile.

Try to avoid taking a full face photograph, where the dog looks into the camera – even the best shaped eye can look full, especially if a flash is used. A three-quarters pose can be very attractive, with the head following the angle.

It looks much better if the handler is out of the picture, but sometimes this is not possible – the dog might become camera shy, or the best photograph may

Ch. Myriehewe Rosa Bleu: Green grass makes a complementary background.
Photo: Russell Fine Art.

be the one with the handler's leg showing. It is annoying, but can be edited out when printed. Memorise the breed Standard, as you do not want to spend a fortune on a well-worded advertisement with the photograph showing the dog's legs following under the chin, the forelegs should be under the withers – anything further forward will denote poor shoulder angulation.

Ch. Lythwood Scrabble, bred and owned by Mr and Mrs Rigby. Different backgrounds can create added interest. *Photo: Diane Pearce.*

Ch. Jazzman Of Janetstown, owned by Mrs J. Moody. Posing front-on for the camera, but retaining a natural look. Photo: Charlotte Clem McGowan.

The perfect combination: A beautifully posed dog against a colourful background.

Remember that Shelties need a neck, and while your Sheltie may look adorable to you when he stares up at your face, it will almost certainly foreshorten the neck and make him look stuffy, at the very least. Try to make him stretch his neck and carry his head proudly.

66

7 THE BREED STANDARD

The aim for all breeders must be to breed a Sheltie that conforms as near as possible to the relevant Standard, and it is our duty to try to breed good quality stock, sound in limb and sensible in temperament.

What is the Standard? Every breed, as recognised by the Kennel Club and the American Kennel Club, has a defined blueprint. It is universally recognised that the country of origin must dictate how the breed should look. It would be no use if people in one country liked a particular characteristic, when people in another country preferred a different one. The breed as we know it would soon become fragmented and, before long, unrecognisable. At the recognition of a breed, a number of enthusiasts get together and literally thrash out the Standard, point by point. It is done in a democratic manner – no one voice should be stronger than the next. Over the years, modifications have been made to the Standard – size being the main

point that has been altered. It is interesting to compare the Standard drawn up by the Kennel Club with the Standard drawn up by the American Shetland Sheepdog Association and approved by the American Kennel Club.

GENERAL APPEARANCE
UK: Small, long-haired working dog of great beauty, free from cloddiness and coarseness. Outline symmetrical, so that no part appears out of proportion to the whole. Abundant coat, mane and frill, shapeliness of head and sweetness of expression combine to present the ideal.

USA: The Shetland Sheepdog is a small, alert, rough coated, long-haired working dog. He must be sound, agile and sturdy. The outline should be so symmetrical that no part appears out of proportion to the whole. Dogs should appear masculine, bitches feminine.

If both paragraphs are read and digested, there are subtle differences. The UK Kennel Club allows no reference to another breed, and stresses that no cloddiness or coarseness can be acceptable, whereas the American Kennel Club Standard calls for sturdiness. These are only small variations, but it shows that, in the UK, we are looking for a Sheltie of 'Toonie' origins, whilst in the USA, we are looking for a sturdy dog resembling a small Rough Collie.

Even after all these years I can still recall the buzz I felt when seeing Colonel Russell's Shelties, standing quietly by their master's side, waiting to cross the road. It was this initial reaction that drew me to the breed; there can be no doubt that the general appearance of a breed is the point of first attraction.

CHARACTERISTICS
UK: Alert, intelligent, strong and active.

USA: There is no mention of characteristics.

TEMPERAMENT
UK: Affectionate and responsive to his owner, reserved towards strangers, never nervous.

USA: The Shetland Sheepdog is intensely loyal, affectionate and responsive to his owner. However, he may be reserved towards strangers but not to the point of showing fear or cringing in the ring.

No-one could argue with either version on this point. Breeders have been successful in improving Sheltie temperament above all else. I am often wary of people setting out to 'improve a breed', as this usually means exaggeration of a particular point. In my early years I was very aware that temperament was a failing in the breed, nervousness was thought one of the breed characteristics. Now, we can hold our heads up proudly, as Shelties are no longer thought of as nervous, and are probably one of the sweetest natural breeds. No-one admires a showing statue, and we like to see a certain amount of inquisitiveness in the breed when in the show ring, but the dog that backs away from the judge can not expect an award in today's competition.

HEAD AND SKULL
UK: Head refined: when viewed from top or side a long, blunt wedge, tapering from ear to nose. Width of skull in proportion to length of skull and muzzle. Whole to be considered in connection with the size of dog. Skull flat, moderately wide between ears, with no prominence of occipital bone. Cheeks flat, merging smoothly into well rounded muzzle. Skull and muzzle of equal length, dividing point inner corner of eye. Top line of

skull parallel to top line of muzzle, with slight but definite stop. Nose, lips and eye-rims black. The characteristic expression is obtained by perfect balance and combination of skull and foreface, shape, colour and placement of eyes, correct position and carriage of ears.

USA: Head: The head should be refined and its shape, when viewed from top or side, be a long, blunt wedge tapering slightly from ears to nose, which must be black. Skull and Muzzle: Top of skull should be flat,

Above: Viewed from the side, the skull and muzzle are on two level planes.

Ch. Shelto Sheraleigh (Moonraker From Mistmere – Exbury Larkspur), owned and bred by Mrs D. Moore. A classic example of the desired sweet expression in a Sheltie bitch.

showing no prominence at nuchal crest (the top of the occiput). Cheeks should be flat and should merge smoothly into a well-rounded muzzle. Skull and muzzle should be of equal length, balance point being inner corner of eye. In profile the top line of skull should parallel the top line of muzzle, but on a higher plane due to the presence of a slight but definite stop. Jaws clean and powerful. The deep, well developed underjaws, rounded at chin, should extend to base of nostril. Lips tight. Upper and lower lips must meet and fit smoothly together all the way round. Teeth level and evenly spaced. Scissor bite.

Both Standards give good coverage of the head – more coverage is given to the jaws, and in particular the underjaw, in the USA Standard. I am also pleased with their coverage of the lip line. There is no doubt that the head properties vary across the Atlantic. In the UK, much more attention is paid to expression, obtainable by the oblique set of the eye. It is not easy to describe, but it is instantly recognisable when you

NS Ch. Mondurle's Bannock (Ch. Francehill Andy Pandy – Stationhill Yolanda), owned by Mr and Mrs Helge Lie (Norway). A perfect example of the desired masculine expression.

see it. The US Standard is very explanatory about tight lips and teeth not being visible when the mouth is closed, and I would say that Shelties in North America are very much better on this point. Perhaps it is easier to achieve with such a fill-up of the muzzle. In the UK we are not used to seeing such strength of either foreface or underjaw.

MOUTH

UK: Jaws level, strong with a well developed underjaw. Lips tight. Teeth – sound with a perfect, regular and complete scissor bite, ie upper teeth closely overlapping the lower teeth and set square to the jaws. A full complement of 42 properly placed teeth highly desirable.

USA: No specific paragraph on the mouth, but this subject is well-covered in the list of 'faults' following skull and muzzle: **"short, receding or shallow underjaw, lacking breadth and depth. Overshot or undershot, missing or crooked teeth. Teeth visible when mouth is closed."**

EYES

UK: Medium size, obliquely set, almond shape. Dark brown except in the case of merles where one or both may be blue or blue flecked.

USA: Medium size with dark, almond shaped rims, set somewhat obliquely in skull. Color must be dark, with blue or merle eyes permissible in merles only.

We appear to be in agreement in these

Ch. Seavall Sheen (Ch. Crisanbee Goldsmith At Myriehewe – Seavall Selebity), bred by Mr E. Robinson and co-owned with Mrs J. Hardman. A golden sable with a white blaze that does not affect her sweet expression.

Ch. Milesend Stormwarden (Ch. Tegwel Wild Ways Of Sandwick – Chelmarsh Countess At Milesend), owned and bred by Mr and Mrs G. Miles. Best of Breed Crufts 1998, a quality example of shaded sable. Photo: Hedberg.

two paragraphs! It is strange that the Standards are so similar on this point, because there are differences. It is very hard to achieve that desired almond shape to the eye. I can well remember an eminent American breeder standing at the ring side at a UK Championship show and exclaiming that the British Shelties all looked "chink-eyed"! We are obviously all striving for the same point – of course, almonds vary in size, and in the UK we often see large eyes, though technically they can still be of almond shape. I think the eyes on North American Shelties are probably the smaller.

EARS
UK: Small, moderately wide at base, placed fairly close together on top of skull. In repose, thrown back; when alert brought forward and carried

Ch. Myriehewe Rosa Bleu (Faradale Facination – Vonstry Wedding Belle), bred and owned by Miss I. Beaden. Winner of 34 CCs , five Working Groups Including two at Crufts), and an all breeds Championship Show BIS winner, also Top Dog All Breeds 1995 – the first time a Sheltie has ever achieved such an honour. Rosa Bleu is the joint breed CC recordholder, sharing the honour with Ch. Herds The Helmsman).
Photo: Dalton.

**semi-erect with tips falling forward.
USA: Small and flexible, placed high,
carried three-fourths erect, with tips
breaking forward. When in repose
the ears fold lengthwise and are
thrown back into the frill.**

There is a difference here. I like the
description of 'flexible' in the US
Standard, but definitely prefer the UK's
'semi-erect'. 'Three-fourths' is not far
off being prick. I like both countries
asking for the tips folding forward – in
my early Sheltie years it was almost
normal to see the 'frying pan' ears on
the side of the head, this is another
point that breeders have improved
enormously.

It is one of life's little mysteries to me

Am. Ch. Lakehill Wayanet Miata.   *Photo: Krook.*

that so often a puppy sold as a pet at eight weeks old, with no sign of flying its ears, can be brought back proudly to see the breeder and the ears have pricked. Perhaps you have kept the brother or sister and have had no problem with the ears flying up into the pricked position, but the ones in the litter sold as pets have developed prick ears. To my mind the sweet Sheltie look is spoiled.

NECK

UK: Muscular, well arched, of sufficient length to carry the head proudly.

USA: Neck should be muscular, arched, and of sufficient length to carry the head proudly.

Good, everyone agrees! It is annoying that so many 'stuffy' necks still win prizes, though!

FOREQUARTERS

UK: Shoulders very well laid back. At the withers separated only by vertebrae, but blades sloping outwards to accommodate desired spring of ribs. Shoulder joint well angled. Upper arm and shoulder blade approximately equal in length. Elbow equidistant from ground and withers. Forelegs straight when viewed from front, muscular and clean with strong bone. Pasterns strong and flexible.

USA: From the withers the shoulder blades should slope at a 45 degree angle forward and downward to the shoulder joints. At the withers they are separated only by the vertebra, but they must slope outward sufficiently to accommodate the desired spring of rib. The upper arm should join the shoulder blade at as nearly as possible a right angle. Elbow joint should be equidistant from the ground or from the withers. Forelegs straight viewed from all angles, muscular and clean, and of strong bone. Pasterns very strong, sinewy and flexible. Dewclaws may be removed.

We are almost in agreement! It would be unusual for British breeders to remove dewclaws and my suspicion is that our idea of 'strong bone' is very different from the American concept of strong bone! Remember that cloddiness is a serious fault.

I am sure that many American breeders would consider British Shelties far too light-boned; it is a major difference between the two countries. I think we get used to seeing our own type of Sheltie, and any variation from the norm looks out of place. Personally, I think much of the difference stems right back to general appearance – the UK Sheltie fanciers hark back to the Toonie origins, and US Sheltie fanciers refer to the Collie influence.

BODY

UK: Slightly longer from point of shoulder to bottom of croup than height to withers. Chest deep, reaching to point of elbow. Ribs well sprung, tapering at lower half to allow free play of forelegs and shoulders. Back level, with graceful sweep over the loins; croup slopes gradually to rear.

USA: In over-all appearance the body should appear moderately long as measured from shoulder joint to ischium (rearmost extremity of the pelvic bone) but much of this length is actually due to the proper angulation and breadth of the shoulder and hindquarters, as the back itself should be comparatively short. Chest should be deep, the brisket reaching to point of elbow. The ribs should be well sprung, but flattened at their lower half to allow free play of the foreleg and shoulder. Abdomen moderately tucked up.

This calls for a lot of thought! In the UK one of the most desirable points is the 'fallaway' – that slope over the croup. We cannot tolerate a high-set tail or 'square' look to the topline. My guess would be that a point treasured as adding grace and outline in the UK would be classed as a fault in the USA. The outline is all-important and here I think the mode of judging has influenced the point. In the UK most of

the shows are judged by specialist breeders, and this sweep over the croup adds grace and a look of agility. However, in the USA and Canada, most of the shows, except for the Specialties, are judged by all-rounders, and they expect to see a complete outline; anything sloping away would look foreign.

HINDQUARTERS

UK: Thigh broad and muscular, thigh bones set into pelvis at right angles. Stifle joint has distinct angle, hock joint clean cut, angular, well let down with strong bone. Hock straight when viewed from behind.

USA: There should be a slight arch at the loins, and the croup should slope gradually to the rear. The hip-bone (pelvis) should be set at a 30 degree angle to the spine. The thigh should be broad and muscular. The thighbone should be set into the pelvis at a right angle corresponding to the angle of the shoulder blade and upper arm. Stifle bones join the thighbone and should be distinctly angled at the stifle joint. The over-all length of the stifle should at least equal the length of the thighbone, and preferably should slightly exceed it. Hock joint should be clean cut, angular, sinewy, with good bone and strong ligamentation. The hock (metatarsus) should be short and

straight viewed from all angles. **Dewclaws should be removed.**

I must confess to reading the US Standard on hindquarters several times and find it confusing. The one point that is totally different to the UK version is the "slight arch at the loins". In the UK this would not be tolerated – the topline must be level with that characteristic sweep down over the croup. However, mention is made of a slope to the croup in the US Standard, which is pleasing. When I judged in Canada recently I was impressed with the hindquarters on the majority of exhibits. I do feel that judges in the UK must not be so lenient on weak or cow hocks. Perhaps the low tail carriage here can camouflage a certain number of failings.

FEET
UK: Oval, soles well padded, toes arched and close together.
USA: Feet should be oval and compact with the toes well arched and fitting tightly together, pads deep and tough, nails hard and strong.

The UK Standard makes no mention of the nails. I like the wording of the US version. I am often surprised that judges fail to notice thin or spread feet. It is a pretty point on our breed and should be regarded carefully. It would be sad to lose that oval shape and the arching of the toes.

TAIL
UK: Set low, tapering bone reaches to at least hocks, with abundant hair and slight upward sweep. May be slightly raised when moving but never over the level of back. Never kinked.

USA: The tail should be sufficiently long so that when it is laid along the back edge of the hind legs the last vertebra will reach the hock joint. Carriage of tail at rest is straight down or in a slight upward curve. When the dog is alert the tail is normally lifted, but it should not be curved forward over the back.

There can be no argument with either version. It was put to me that a tail that is carried 'gaily' (higher than the level of the back) is forgivable as long as the tail is not curled. It is a throwback to the Spitz influence early in the Sheltie's origins, and I must say that a curly tail does look totally foreign. A tail carried up looks stilted and aggressive. It is a very important point. In the UK it is absolutely taboo for the tail to be carried gaily; however, UK exhibitors move their dogs more slowly, and a dog will more readily raise his tail when moved faster. I feel that this is another point where the mode of judging has allowed this

Blue-flecked brown eyes are permissable in a blue merle.

Blue eyes are also permissable in a blue merle.
Photo: Downs.

difference between the countries in the show ring.

GAIT AND MOVEMENT
UK: Lithe, smooth and graceful with drive from hindquarters, covering the maximum amount of ground with the minimum of effort. Pacing, plaiting, rolling or stiff, stilted up and down movement highly undesirable.

USA: The trotting gait of the Shetland Sheepdog should denote speed and smoothness. There should be no jerkiness, nor stiff, stilted up-and-down movement. The drive should be from the rear, true and straight dependent upon correct angulation, musculation, and ligamentation of the entire hindquarter, thus allowing the dog to reach well under his body with his

Ch. Cultured At Cashella (Herd's It's Hindsight – Beckwith Bit Of A Dream), bred by Mr and Mrs D. MacMillan, owned by Mr and Mrs P. Johnstone. Best of Breed Crufts 1988, a fine example of a tricolour. Photo: Sally Anne Thompson.

hind foot and propel himself forward. Reach of stride of the foreleg is dependent upon correct angulation, musculation and ligamentation of the forequarters, together with correct width of chest and construction of rib cage. The foot should be lifted only enough to clear the ground as the leg swings forward. Viewed from the front, both forelegs and hindlegs should move forwards almost perpendicular to the ground at the

German Ch. Mossmill Magpie from Valjon. Owners: Ilbeck/Feldhoff.
Black and white is a permitted colour, but it is not often seen in the UK.
Photo: Feldhoff.

walk, slanting a little inward at a slow trot, until at a swift trot the feet are brought so far forward toward center line of body that the tracks left show parallel lines of footprints actually touching a center line at their inner edges. There should be no crossing of the feet nor throwing of the weight from side to side.

The list of faults in the US Standard covers the same faults as the UK Standard, so we all seem to agree. I am surprised that there is no mention in the UK Standard of the feet being kept low, as we love the term 'daisy-cutting' action!

The subject of movement/gait is very well covered in the US version. This is possibly why the show dogs are moved at a different pace to show dogs in the UK. It is certainly true that the movement of the North American Sheltie denotes speed; any UK judge will be surprised at the speed with which the exhibits are moved. They look very impressive, and I know that movement is a particularly important part of the American and Canadian show scene. However, it is not to be assumed that movement in the UK show ring is not important, because it is, but emphasis is put on the smoothness and effortlessness and not on speed. One interesting feature is that I can see no mention in the UK Standard of 'single tracking', whereas this is very well described in the US version.

COAT

UK: Double; outer coat of long hair, harsh textured and straight. Undercoat soft, short and close. Mane and frill abundant, forelegs well feathered. Hindlegs above hocks profusely covered with hair, below hocks fairly smooth. Face smooth. Smooth coated specimens highly undesirable.

USA: The coat should be double, the outer coat consisting of long, straight, harsh hair; the undercoat short, furry, and so dense as to give the entire coat its 'stand-off' quality. The hair on face, tips of ears and feet should be smooth. Mane and frill should be abundant, and particularly impressive on males. The forelegs well feathered, the hindlegs heavily so, but smooth below the hock joint. Hair on tail profuse. Note: excess hair on ears, feet, and on hocks may be trimmed for the show ring.

The wording is a little different but the meaning is the same in both Standards. The US Standard also mentions smooth specimens in its list of faults, and that soft, wavy, silky or curly coats are counted as incorrect. We certainly agree!

COLOURS

UK: SABLES: Clear or shaded, any colour from pale gold to deep mahogany, in its shade, rich in tone. Wolf sable or grey undesirable.
TRICOLOURS: Intense black on body, rich tan markings preferred.
BLUE MERLES: Clear, silvery blue, splashed and marbled with black. Rich tan markings preferred but absence not penalised. Heavy black markings, slate or rusty tinge in either top or undercoat highly undesirable; general effect must be blue.
BLACK & WHITE and BLACK & TAN are also recognised colours. White markings may appear (except on black & tan) in blaze, collar and chest, frill, legs and tip of tail. All or some white markings are preferred

(except on black & tan) and absence of these markings not to be penalised. Patches of white on body highly undesirable.

USA: Black, blue merle, and sable (ranging from golden through mahogany); marked with varying amounts of white and/or tan.

FAULTS: Rustiness in a black or blue coat. Washed out or degenerate colors, such as pale sable or faded blue. Self-color in the case of blue merle, that is, without any merling or mottling and generally appearing as a faded or dilute tricolor. Conspicuous white body spots. Specimens with more than 50% white shall be so severely penalized as to effectively eliminate them from competition.

DISQUALIFICATION: Brindle.

I felt it prudent to include the whole paragraph on faults relating to colour. It would be absolutely taboo for a white or mismark to be exhibited in the UK. I wonder when it became permissible for even 50% of white to enter the American show ring. I have noticed that many more are exhibited with white blazes in the USA – some twenty or thirty years ago blazes became very unfashionable in the UK, partly, I feel, due to the strong influence of the Misses Rogers of the Riverhill Kennels. They were often heard to voice disapproval of white on the face, and some of the Riverhill expressions were exquisite. Now we seem to have returned to the days of accepting white on the face as normal – in fact the well-known Ch. Seavall Sheen is a very worthy exponent of not only a blaze, but an unsymmetrical blaze at that, and no one could criticise her on expression! There is no doubt that the sable colouring varies across the Atlantic – in the UK we love pale goldens and orange reds, but we do not see a lot of the deep mahogany colours that are quite normal in the USA. Americans seem much more adventurous over colour matings, whereas in the UK we are totally traditional! I am envious of their lovely quality black & whites; we seldom see a black & white in the UK, but interest in this colour has grown in recent years. We also seldom see a blue merle without tan. The rich tan is considered part of the rich hue of the blue merle – I am not saying that a blue merle without tan would be penalised in the show ring, but, all points being equal, the one with tan would be preferred.

SIZE
UK: Ideal height at the withers: Dogs 37 cm (14.4 in) Bitches 35.5 cm (14 in). More than 2.5 cm (1 in) above or below these heights highly undesirable.

USA: The Shetland Sheepdog should stand between 13 and 16 inches at the shoulder. Note: Height is determined by a line perpendicular to the ground from the top of the shoulder blades, the dog standing naturally, with forelegs parallel to line of measurement. Heights below or above the desired size range are to be disqualified from the show ring.

Obviously there is a small difference here, as the USA Standard allows up to 16 inches, whereas the UK Standard has no maximum. Indeed the same can be said for the minimum, but the ideal height is the aim of breeders in the UK. It can be truly said that the interpretation of this is in the judge's eye – and no one is perfect! It is a dilemma to be faced with a lovely sound dog that is over the height ideal, and another of perfect size but not so well-made. Who would be a judge!

ENTIRETY
UK two apparently normal testicles fully descended into the scrotum.

USA: non-entirety is a disqualification, as it is in most other countries.

In the UK, non-entirety is regarded as a fault, but in fact non-entire dogs can be exhibited. Whether they win or not is at the discretion of the judge. In the UK we can also breed with a dog that is not entire, which surprises a lot of breeders in other countries. My personal view is that it is hard enough to breed a winner, let alone risk perpetuating monorchidism!

8 THE SHOW RING

As discussed in Chapter Six (Training Your Sheltie), a lot of hard work goes into training your puppy for the show ring, and it may be some months before you feel ready for that first show. When that time comes, the first step is finding out about the shows in your area. There are several dog magazines that list the shows, and the shows are advertised well in advance. Rather than jumping off at the deep end by attending a major Championship show, why not enter at a small, local event and get the feel of what it's all about. Look down the list of shows and choose one that takes place when the puppy is over six months old – this is the minimum age at which you can legally show, although it probably would be sensible to wait until he is a little more mature. The entry form can be obtained with the schedule from the show secretary, and the appropriate fee has to be sent. Why

not try just one class at first and use this first outing as practise?

PREPARATION

Before the day of the show, you will need to bath the puppy and this will be easy – you have already learned that lesson number one was to make him stand still when you say "stand".

You will need to take some equipment with you, and I would suggest that you check against this list:
Sports bag or hold-all
Collar, check-chain and lead
Show lead
Brush and two combs
Blanket
Crate (if you have one, and you will regret it if you do not)
Ring number clip
Your puppy's favourite tidbit
Small bowl for water
Small plastic bottle of water.
Also, it will be a good idea to take some water in a spray bottle to freshen up his

coat, and a towel in case he gets wet or grubby going from car park to the showground – be prepared for wet weather if it is an outdoor event! You will need to buy a catalogue to find your ring number and also to see the opposition.

ON THE DAY

I would advise that you arrive early to allow yourself and the puppy time to settle. Ask the people on the gate where Shelties are to be judged, and then take yourself to the ringside. Keep your eye on the ring where the judging will take place. A steward will arrive to put up a notice board and to supervise generally. A few minutes before the time of judging, another steward will arrive with the judging book, the relevant cards and rosettes, and is often accompanied by the judge of the day. Your entrant by this time will be fully groomed, his show lead is on and he is enjoying the anticipation of that tidbit

in your pocket. You will need to have the ring number clip on the left of your chest for the steward to see clearly. The numbers will be called into the ring – and if you have entered for the puppy class, you will probably be in the first class. It is your responsibility to get into the right class – if in doubt, ask the steward on entry.

I would not recommend that you are the first person in. Procedure differs country to country, but my advice is to let one or two of the more seasoned exhibitors go before you, watch them and follow.

IN THE RING

Sometimes the judge will send all the exhibitors round the ring and ask them to stop and 'show' while he takes a cursory look before asking for the first dog to set up on the table. Observe how the first exhibit is moved, because the judge may ask for a triangle or for two straight up-and-down laps. Sometimes

The author judging bitches in the National Working Breeds Show 1991. Photo: Sundbye.

Francehill Gold Venture: When assessing the head, look for a long, blunt wedge.
Photo: Haslett.

the judge will move to the side to ascertain the quality of the puppy's movement from the side. Do not get yourself in a muddle by swapping hands at the last minute. Dogs are shown in the left hand. On your way back toward the judge, he will want to see the exhibit brought to a stop to show. This will be well under control because you have been practising this routine at home. Try to ascertain the best place to stop – if you are too close, the judge will get a good view of the top of the dog's head and back, whereas if you come to a stop a fair distance from the judge, he should get a good view of the dog's profile and his beautifully arched neck. This is the moment you have worked towards, so it is only common sense to try to make your dog look as good as possible.

Some judges stand and make notes; other judges may ask you to move again – perhaps you were not going at the right pace. Usually, after what seems like a lifetime, the judge will say "thank you", and you should then go back in line to your original position. Do praise your dog – not so much to get him so excited that his tail flies up, but enough to keep his interest. Reward him with a tidbit.

When the judge has examined all the exhibits in the class, he will walk round to check the expression and stance of each exhibit. It is absolutely taboo to crowd too close to the person in front;

try to allow a little space between your dog and the one either side. Keep your dog's concentration – this is easy because you have practised at home! Nothing can be more annoying than to have someone beside you desperate to get their dog's ears brought to attention by throwing tidbits to the floor. It is not fair on other competitors, and it looks amateurish.

When I first started showing, I was

Ch. Our Barny of Edglonian showing the flat skull and rounded foreface that is typical of the breed. Photo: Pearson.

quite a young girl. I can well remember some breeders (who I had read about and regarded somewhere in the same category as one would regard a Greek god) who had not done their homework, or who had nervous dogs, having to resort to drastic measures to get their dogs' attention. Nowadays we do not see the plethora of balls, fluffy toys or sqeakers that used to be hurled in front of those reluctant show dogs!

Having established that your dog will be beautifully behaved, keep an eye on the judge. He may well not speak, but may just point at you to bring your dog out. If this happens, give an encouraging squeeze on the lead, promise a reward and move proudly out. Concentrate, as this may well be the first 'cut', where the judge's choices are called into the middle of the ring and the outer circle will be politely told "thank you". If you are one of the outer circle, retire quickly and sit and watch the finalisation of the class. Luckily, Shelties can sit on your knee while you follow the proceedings, although you may want to mark the catalogue. However, if you are kept in the ring for further consideration, then do not relax, but keep your dog's attention on that promised tidbit, as you can never tell when he might catch the judge's eye. There will be five dogs placed, and the judge will move along the line with the steward and hand out the prize cards.

If you are first or second, the judge will ask you to stay while he writes a critique before you leave the ring. The winner will be recalled at the conclusion of all the Sheltie classes to compete for the Best of Breed award, and, following this, there could be a further rosette for Best Puppy in Breed.

There may well have been a specialist judge who was only judging Shelties, so if you get a chance, you could ask him what he thought of your dog or your performance. If, however, it is one of the many all-round judges, he may not get the chance to chat with you, because as soon as the Sheltie classes are finished, he will be starting on his next breed.

It is a wonderful feeling when you win that first prize card, and it can be the encouragement you needed to begin a lifetime's hobby.

SHOWING IN THE USA

In the USA, Champions (or 'specials') are generally shown only in a seperate class to compete for Best of Breed (and from there, placings in group or even Best in Show), but does not normally influence the competition for Championship points. This is not actually a rule, but it is definitely expected that the owner of a dog who finishes a Championship will 'move the dog up' and show in Specials at the next show. This type of move can be made up to half an hour before the start of judging at any show.

Non-champions may be entered in any of several classes, all divided by sex:

Puppy (often divided by age), 12 - 18 months, Novice, Bred by Exhibitor, American Bred, and Open. Any class may be divided by colour. The dogs who are undefeated in these classes are then judged with others of the same sex to determine the Winners Dog and Winners Bitch. These two will get the points allotted to that show (between 0 and 5 points, with points for dogs and bitches determined separately), and will also be allowed to compete with the Specials (US Champions) for Best of Breed status. The American Shetland Sheepdog Association allows use of the title CC (Century Club) for a dog with 100 or more Best of Breed wins, and 2CC (200 club) for a dog with 200 or more.

To become a US Ch, a dog must accumulate at least 15 points under three judges, and at least two of the shows at which points are won must be 'majors' – shows offering three or more points won under two different judges. The number of points awarded at any show is based on the number of dogs competing and on the region in which the show is held, but the AKC attempts to set the point rating (the relationship between number of dogs shown and points available) so that about 20% of the shows in each region are majors. In 1997, for instance, there were 1,387 AKC shows in the US. 235 of these shows offered majors for dogs, and 233 did for bitches. The actual number of majors awarded was higher, as at a show where there is a major for one sex but not the other, if the dog winning the lower rating goes Best of Winners both winners get the major points. 237 Champions finished in 1997, suggesting that most majors go to dogs who do win their Championships.

A dog who wins Best of Breed competes with other herding dogs for first, second, third and fourth in the herding group. The first place dog in each group goes on to compete for Best in Show. Note that in the USA, the herding group was split off from the working group in 1983. The herding group includes only the herders; flock guard dogs such as the Komondor, the Kuvasz, and the Great Pyrenees remain in the working group.

Although there are still many owners who show their own dogs in the United States, the winning dogs are often handled and groomed by professionals. As one result, the dogs who are most likely to win at US shows are often the very showy, 'up' dogs with ears continuously on the top of the head, who naturally or through training stack themselves into a 'show pose'. Another trend is toward a coat that is easy to style (trimming and brushing legally, texturizers, and dyes illegally) rather than the correct, easy-to-care-for care coat. The use of white chalk as a grooming aid is permitted, but it must be completely removed before the dog enters the ring. Another factor that helps make presentation so important in the

United States is that although prospective judges must (among other requirements) have bred two US Champions, many all-breed judges started out as handlers rather than breeders.

JUDGING SYSTEMS

There are virtually two systems of judging – in the UK, North America and Australasia the class is judged on merit, the best one winning a first, the second best is second, and so on. The exhibits are compared against each other.

In many countries, Fédération Cynologique Internationale (FCI) rules apply. Each dog is judged against the breed Standard, a written report is given on each exhibit, then the judge grades them as Excellent, Very Good, Good, etc. Those given Excellent come back in the ring to be placed first to fourth. As you can imagine, it takes a considerable while and the poor steward whose task it is to do all that writing really works hard.

However boring it is to watch, there are merits in the system, and at least everybody knows just what the judge thinks of their exhibit. It would be wholly unworkable in the UK, where we are used to such large entries, even just taking notes on the first two placings takes a while.

BECOMING A JUDGE

You may decide that you would like to judge in due course, and before deciding you really must ask yourself why! Why should you want to give up a day, stand in the centre of a show ring (probably in the rain!) and at the end of it, have to take criticism? If it is to boost the old ego, then perhaps you ought to rethink the whole thing. Maybe the thought of getting revenge on Joe Bloggs, who was stupid enough not to place your dog at a previous show, might be the lure! It is an honour to be invited to judge, and personally I think the only approach from the start should be a feeling of being able to contribute to the dog scene – to give something back instead of always receiving. Often the decisions are close and you must be able to stand criticism – once you are in the centre of the ring you are being judged by both exhibitors and spectators on your decisions.

JUDGING YOUR FIRST SHOW

Having accepted your first appointment, the day of the show draws close. You will have received confirmation from the secretary, with a schedule and details of your entries. The secretary will have asked you to be there at a specific time and my advice is to arrive half an hour early – you must report to the secretary's office and collect your envelope with your judging book, often a rosette to pin on your jacket saying 'judge', and possibly a luncheon ticket. You will be told which ring your breed will be in, and about five minutes before you are scheduled to start, you can go to the ring and get yourself settled. Try not to be nervous, but on the other hand, do not engage in jolly conversation with the exhibitors. You will probably have two ring stewards, and they should look after you. One will see to the secretarial work, and the other will marshal the dogs in and give out ring numbers.

IN THE RING

As the class lines up, take a careful look at them all. If space allows, it would be nice to have them circle the ring a couple of times. You will be expected to stand in the centre and have them go round in an anti-clockwise direction so that all the entrants can be seen clearly – most people hold the lead in their left hand. Do not make the mistake of turning to watch them as they pass – if you stay fairly static you will get the chance to see every exhibit moving. The more experienced handlers will move with that bit of panache, whereas the less experienced might make all sorts of mistakes!

It is your job to find out why each one is moving as it does, and this you will do with the examination each exhibit will receive on the table. Stop them moving around the ring at the same place that the line started, and ask for the first exhibit to set up on the table. You must give each one the same examination – start off with a check on the teeth, then examine the head and underjaw. Check the ears, then progress along the dog: neck, set and angulation

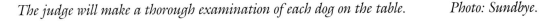

The judge will make a thorough examination of each dog on the table.   *Photo: Sundbye.*

With a longcoated breed, it is important to get beneath the coat and assess construction. Photo: Sundbye.

of shoulder, elbows, bone, front and feet. Then feel the topline; the required brisket will be shallow because it is, after all, a puppy class. Feel the croup and hind angulation. Do not be content to just measure the tail against the hock for length; feel along it in case there is a kink, and feel that it is set right. While it is not wise to take too long, it is worth that bit of extra time, as it will help to settle you into a routine. Note the exhibitor's number, and if you feel that there is something worth noting down (the puppy in question might not be entire) then you are perfectly within your rights to make a note of it in either the margin of your judging book, or in your own notebook if you have one.

Then request that the exhibit is moved. Personally, I hate triangles – there is usually not the room for a moving breed like a Sheltie to get in its stride before it has to turn into the next stage of the triangle. If you feel the same, then send the puppy the full length of the ring, noting the movement behind. It might take a few strides before he is gaiting smoothly. The journey back to you will reveal a lot about the puppy's front assembly. Remember the Standard – no 'jerky up and down movement'. If you feel unsure, ask the exhibitor to move again. Many people are so anxious for the dog to stand and show its ears that movement is virtually forgotten. You will have seen side movement when the exhibits first went round the ring, but you can always ask for a second gaiting while you stand to the side. It is only fair that everybody has the same opportunity to show off their dog, and it is only courteous for the judge to give every exhibitor the same time to assess their dog's virtues.

THE JUDGE'S CHOICE

When you have gone over every exhibit in this, your first class, all will stand for your final decision. Walk along the line slowly, and remember that you are judging how they appear before you on that day – no one has the right to look into the crystal ball to see how they will look when adult!

Once you have made a decision, then pull your selection into the centre of the ring. There are usually five prize cards at British shows, so if possible choose five. This is not always possible – in a large class, it might be necessary to select more than five to make your final decision. Let's hope you do not want six from which to make your final selection, as this will mean that just one will be cardless. However, the important thing is to get the selection right and if this means reassessing six, then so be it.

Once you are sure in your mind, then pull out your first and so on down the line. It is best to place them in a

prominent position in the centre of the ring; the first prize winner should be on your left and the rest of the line should follow suit. Try to face them to the ringside, so people can see the numbers and mark their catalogues. The judging book is to be collected from the judge's table – sometimes the steward will bring this to you when they collect the prize cards to distribute. British judges will notice that the two serrated strips on the right-hand side of the page need filling in with the numbers, and the inner margin is for the judge to mark or make comments in! The serrated strips are to be removed and handed to the steward – these then go to the secretary's table. You make notes on the first placed dog as this will form part of your written critique. The steward in the meantime will be calling the numbers for the next class. If there are any 'old' dogs in this class they will be placed one side of the ring and the 'new' exhibits will be lined up as before.

I do not know another country where it is usual to enter in several classes, but this means that once you have gone over an exhibit, you do not need to have it placed on the table again, though you might well want to refresh your memory and move some of them again. Judge the new class in exactly the same way as you did the first, except that you must remember to reassess the 'already seen' exhibits.

When you have judged all your classes, the class winners are called into the ring for you to give the Best of Breed award, and it is imperative that you send the best representative forward as your Best of Breed. Your reputation will be built on this decision, as by giving this award you are declaring it to be the nearest to the breed Standard that you have found. There may well be an award for Best Puppy, and this need not necessarily come from the puppy class, as someone with two puppies may have entered one in the puppy class and one in a subsequent class.

Once you have completed your judging you may speak to the exhibitors. Try not to sound timid by asking "How did I do?", but do not be too boastful either! Thank your stewards. If you have been given a luncheon ticket, perhaps suggest that they join you – this may not be possible if they are stewarding for other judges. There is no doubt about it, you will have learned a lot!

It is best not to have a great post-mortem on your decisions, if you feel you made some mistakes then learn by them rather than go round apologising to exhibitors as this will not instil confidence in you or your decisions.

A GOOD JUDGE

What makes a good judge? Can a person learn to be a judge, or are you born with an instinct for quality – having an 'eye'? The most honest person in the world might not make a good judge, and I suppose the reverse could be said, that a good judge might not always make an honest decision. If the latter were to happen, then those at the ringside would soon know, and the general 'feel' of the show will be marred. It would even reflect in the size of the entry next time that particular judge officiated.

It is debatable which is better, the specialist judge or the all-breeds judge. The specialist is bound to be slower; they must have a deep knowledge of the breed, but could be accused of fault judging and being adamant about breed type as against soundness. The all-rounder is quicker, slicker and probably more professional in his or her approach; one would expect soundness and construction to be important points. At one time, it was thought that you had to show a glamorous 'showing fool' to catch the all-rounder's eye, but I do not think that can be said of today's judges.

JUDGING ABROAD

The UK Kennel Club has a reciprocal agreement with many other countries – a judge qualified in another country will automatically qualify in the UK. This seems fair to an extent, but grossly unfair in another way. A judge from a country where Shelties are not numerous may have had hands-on experience with very few specimens. Yet, because of the exam to judge breeds within a group he or she has qualified as a Championship show judge. An up-

and-coming judge in the UK has had to have judged at least 100 dogs before being considered experienced enough to even sit an exam – and that only qualifies them for the lower (Open shows) judges lists! More experience, and possibly a breed club Open show, would be needed to qualify for Championship status.

There is no doubt, the UK judge is the most experienced – sometimes the apprenticeship has lasted half a lifetime. In North America, as already mentioned, the majority of shows are judged by all-breeds judges, and with the plethora of shows they are in constant demand and are very experienced. Like the UK judge, the all-breeds judge from the USA and Canada has a wealth of experience, and they are in demand to officiate at shows around the world.

9 BREEDING SHELTIES

When I was a girl my family were appalled at the thought of me being a dog breeder and I must say that in retrospect, I agree with their sentiments! Why on earth one should want to be a dog breeder is a mystery, and yet…

DECIDING TO BREED
To be a breeder requires a certain amount of energy, devotion and enthusiasm. If you are embarking on your first litter, you must face the possibility of things going wrong, the heartbreak of either losing puppies, or your bitch having to have a Caesarean section, or even whelping a lovely healthy litter, only to find that there are mismarks among them. Even worse is the possibility of something being wrong with the puppies themselves, such as a cleft palate or deformity.

Puppies are adorable, and such fun when they are clean, but that cleanliness

Ch. Felthorn Lady, Ch. Felthorn Cornflower and Ch. Felthorn Our Kate: Three generations of homebred blue merle champion bitches. Our Kate produced Ch. Felthorn Genevieve At Dellahill, making a record four tail female blue merles. bred by Mr and Mrs Thornley.

can only be achieved by constantly washing their box, the floors, putting down clean papers and bedding, to say nothing of brushing each puppy, keeping it's nails short, feeding and washing bowls all day long. You are not allowed a day off; after all, they are your puppies – why should your husband, daughter or neighbour have to clean them, while you enjoy the luxury of being ill with the 'flu?

Bringing a litter of puppies into the world is a big responsibility, not just while they are in your care, but as a back-up for the rest of the puppies' lives. After all, haven't you sought the advice of the breeder who bred their mother? Make sure that you have the stamina for all of this.

I hope that I am not coming across as a scaremonger, I actually enjoy kennel work, and the joy of seeing a healthy, happy litter playing contentedly still gives me a feeling of satisfaction, and that is after 45 years of Sheltie breeding.

ASSESSING THE BITCH

Having questioned your motives for wanting a litter and your dedication to care for the puppies, you must look at your bitch with an unbiased eye. To my mind, there are only two totally essential criteria to look for in the breeding bitch – temperament and health. The old idea that having a litter will make the nervous bitch more steady is out with the ark – you will only achieve in bringing another four or five

similar temperaments into the world. The same goes for bitches who are aggressive or frightened of their own shadows.

To breed from a bitch knowing that she is not 100% in health is beyond comment. I would suggest that any history of fits, skin trouble, slipping patella, deafness, blindness or kidney disease must rule out the possibility of breeding from the affected animal, or its relatives.

Even the most successful kennels in the show ring sell the majority of their puppies into private, pet homes, and if your bitch is a joy and delight to you, then if you choose a suitable dog to breed her with, you will succeed in making several other people as happy as you have been!

Having ascertained that your bitch is healthy in mind and limb, the next step is to study her as objectively as you can, because the choice of stud dog is all-important.

THE RIGHT STUD DOG

The best way to choose a suitable mate is by your own eye and judgement, although it seems almost heresy to say it, but more harm can be done by trying to 'linebreed' and 'keep in pedigree' when you are not really au fait with the situation.

If your bitch has a round eye, then common sense must dictate that her mate must have the desired almond-shaped eye. If you have trouble with

Ch. Tegwel Wildways Of Sandwick (Ch. Lythwood Skymaster – Marklin Wild Gipsy Of Tegwel): Top stud dog all breeds for 1997 – a truly remarkable achievement. Bred by Mr and Mrs Stanley, owned by Mr and Mrs Mayhew.

either pricked or heavy ears, then look at the dogs' ears before deciding.

Go through your bitch point by point, and select your choice of stud dog while assessing her faults against his good points. The best place to see a good selection of dogs is at a dog show. Many dog magazines give full listings of forthcoming shows, and if you can make it to a Championship show, then so much the better. My advice is always to go for the best possible stud dog, and these will not be found at the local events. Breeders like to show their best stock at Championship level.

There will be a lot of classes to watch. The dog judging will take place in the morning and while the first two or three classes will be interesting, your choice of stud is more likely to come from the mature classes. The top winners are usually to be found among the Champions and near Champions. With the big entries, there will be ample time to sit and study form; check your catalogue to see the age and breeding of the dogs that take your fancy. The distance to be travelled to the show really is secondary to the right choice of stud dog. Bear in mind that some people are much better handlers than others, and inevitably the dog handled to advantage is bound to look a better prospect, but has he that long tail that you must have, or the ears, or the movement?

If you see a dog that pleases you and he has the good points that your bitch does not have, then wait until the class is over and the dog put back on his bench, and approach the owner. Most people are pleased that you have selected their dog as a possibility, but not every dog is at public stud for various reasons. It could prove that the dog you wanted is not at stud, so try to make a shortlist and have a look at them all. It is unfair to the dog and the owner

Ch. Glaysdale Heiress and Ch. Glaysdale Buccaneer (Ch. Francehill Andy Pandy – Greensands Glad Eye). Bred by Jackie Harrison (owner of Heiress), and Buccaneer is owned by Isobel Davidson. Both winning their third CC at the Yorkshire Shetland Sheepdog Club.

99

to automatically handle the dog on the bench, much better to ask the owner first. Anything that is shy or aggressive on the bench must be avoided like the plague – temperament is inherited through both sides of the pedigree.

It could happen that you have seen nothing that excites you, in which case do not be rushed. There are plenty of shows, and after all this is going to be laying the foundation of your stock.

THE BROOD BITCH

Just supposing that you have found the dog of your choice and that he is at public stud. You have tentatively made the arrangement to use him and will notify the owner as soon as your bitch comes in season. This can seem a lifetime! Shelties are not a breed to come in season to order – some of mine go months over their expected time. I find that once one shows signs of coming in season, then the others follow suit, almost as if it were catching!

The onset of season varies from one bitch to another. They seem more attention-seeking, especially in the case of a young maiden bitch, and no doubt the observant owner will notice a tightening of the stomach. The following day could see the start of a 'colour show' – this is often dark and somewhat brackish to begin with. The season may be preceded by a delicate licking. Inspection will show that the vulva is swollen, but still no sign of colour, and sometimes there can be several days before the colour actually shows. The best time to look for it is first thing in the morning.

The time to contact the stud dog owner is when you are sure that it is a 'colour show' – there is no use ringing until you are sure. There may be other people wanting to use the same dog, so while there is no panic, it is only sensible to notify the stud dog owner once colour is beyond doubt.

Now, if your bitch has had a season before, the chances are that you will have noticed when she became 'flirty' – usually from 12 to 15 days after the first onset of colour. These first few days are no trouble, but as the vulva enlarges she will give off a scent to encourage any males, and it is the responsibility of the owner of the bitch to keep her safe. Unless it is impossible to restrict her to garden exercise, I would only take her out of her home environment if absolutely necessary. Even in your garden, do not forget that neighbours' dogs could try to jump in, so while it is not for long, perhaps you should keep her under your watchful eye!

I usually tell 'my girls' that it is 'purdah' for the next two to three weeks, and when it is walk-time for everybody else, the bitches in season can stay at home and have an extra 'chew'.

After the first week she should be quite swollen but still colouring, and the top of the vulva will still feel hard, though as the days pass she should

Five generations of Lythwood Champion dogs (left to right): Ch. Lythwood Saga, Ch. Lythwood Spruce, Ch. Lythwood Scrabble, Ch. Lythwood Steptoe, and Ch. Brandy Snap (front) – a unique record in the breed.

soften up. They really can vary a lot, and just because she is flirting with your other bitches does not mean that she will necessarily 'stand' for a dog. When she has reached her peak it would be wise to phone the stud owner and report proceedings. You will have given an approximation when you rang to say that colour had started. This soft swollen state lasts for a few days, and usually the colour will have eased off, finally turning watery. By this time she should react to pressure or a little tickling. If she is going to be receptive she will start to ripple her back and flag her tail to one side in an unmistakable manner. A lot of breeders 'feel' the bitch internally, and while this has to be done prior to some matings, I am against any sort of intervention unless necessary. Germs are only too happy to find a way in! Of course if the mating does not take place with ease, then nature may need a small helping hand but do not cross that bridge unless you have to.

When the big day arrives it is important that your bitch is taken in a clean condition – common courtesy costs nothing. I like to bath mine prior to mating anyway. Hopefully you will have a crate in which to travel her, if at all possible try to let her urinate before she is presented to the dog. Usually this is no problem as a bitch in season likes to broadcast the fact. A request always made from someone breeding for the first time is to allow the two to play together. In an ideal world the mating would be a love match, they would romp under the apple blossom and a 'tie' would be accomplished unaided. Dream on – it rarely happens like that!

THE MATING

While it is in everybody's interest for the mating to occur quickly and easily, you will find that after the initial greeting, you will be expected to take hold of your bitch by the collar. The stud dog owner will have a quick look to determine that she really is in season, and will then 'part the petticoats' and hold her rear end while encouraging the dog to mount. Most stud dogs are trained to mount straight away and your bitch may well object to being suddenly mounted, so hold tight and do not let her turn and take a snap at him. He will probably dismount, check with his owner, and be encouraged again. This time he means business, and after a few preliminary pushes he will work rapidly until he feels secure in a holding position. It is important to hold your bitch firmly during this time. Try not to keep chattering, as the stud owner will be concentrating on the dog, making sure that he is fully extended inside and

holding him secure for a few minutes before releasing his front legs to the floor, so that their two heads are facing the same way. Once sure that the dog is secure and that the bitch is steady, one of his hind legs will be gently lifted over so the two will be back to back. It looks an unbelievable position but it is nature's way of acting as a 'stopper' and this 'tie' can last from five to 30 minutes. Your bitch may react with some moans and wriggles; do not distract her as they are both best left to their own thoughts. However, continue to hold her collar, for once the tie has ended it is a wise precaution to raise her rear end up, trying to keep the sperm in place for as long as possible. Then carry her to her crate in the car. She has earned your praise, and a rest, while you have a well earned cup of tea. You will be expected to pay the stud fee at the time of mating, and in return, you will be given a copy of the dog's pedigree and there will be some paperwork to complete in order that the litter can be registered with the national Kennel Club when the puppies are born. Check with your national Kennel Club so that you know what is required.

THE DIFFICULT STUD DOG

One of my very few grumbles about Shelties is that they are not always successful as stud dogs. Why this should be is really a bit of a mystery – they are a nice 'natural' breed with no deformities (such as short legs, short pump-handle tails or excessive fat), but so often we hear the old tale "he just won't mate!". People seem to think that just because they are dogs they will mate automatically, no matter what, but having had stud dogs that ranged from brilliant to useless, I thought a few helpful tips might save a bit of blood pressure on the owner's part!

Taking it for granted that the bitch is absolutely 'spot on', the stud dog should be instantly interested, and after the initial introduction and foreplay he should mount her and start working. But this does not always happen, and there are several things that can be done to help. Should the dog not penetrate on attempting, the bitch must be thoroughly examined. You should take her away from the dog, and once you have scrubbed your hands clean, she should be examined internally with a lightly greased finger. Even though swollen on the outside, the vagina may have a stricture, which will probably break with gentle but firm manipulation. It could be that the vagina itself is tiny, and it is surprising how effective just working a well-greased finger into it will help.

However, if the bitch stands there rippling her back, with ears alert and tail flagging, only to find that the dog yawns and walks away, you have another problem altogether. You can try several ways to stimulate his interest. Lift the bitch up, and saying "goodbye" to the unwilling partner, start for the door, even taking her right away for a few minutes and starting again. If he is sniffing and licking at her, but making no effort to mount, try rolling her over gently on her back. This can have a magic effect and he will often try to mount before she is back up on her legs again. Alternatively, lift her hind legs up, so her rear is out of reach; this usually gets him standing up on his hind legs to try to reach, and if you are quick you can lower her quickly under him.

Several times I have been asked to help with a mating when the dog will show interest but keeps grasping either the end of her tail or one hind leg, and works away like fury, going nowhere fast. You should always stop this as it is a waste of your time and his sperm. Try to get him to start again by teasing him into mounting her, but this time make sure that the bitch is backed up fairly close to a solid wall, or into a corner, even easing her back so that he is forced to place both front legs round her waist. Once he has the idea that he has to grip her securely, he should react and work closely.

The most difficult stud dog is one who refuses to mount. You have to start him off, but this is a last resort method, as once the dog finds you working on his behalf he will often expect this treatment each time. If you have a 'refuse to mount' situation, it is virtually impossible to manage on your own, so a colleague is needed, not only to hold the bitch but to hold fast the dog's two front legs. He will need to be backed against a solid wall, and the bitch backed alongside him. Then, lifting him up, straddle his two front legs in the 'waist' position. He will often try to struggle free, so keep calm, and start working him with one hand, pressing lightly but firmly with quick strokes on his sheath. Do not pull him forward, in fact if you rhythmically stroke him backwards, he will start to jerk forward of his own accord. With your other hand under the bitch's vulva, you will be able to guide the now extended penis into her, but keep working the dog with increased activity until he is fully inside the bitch. Hold him on until you are sure he is in the 'tie' position, and even then do not be in any hurry to release the front legs from the 'waist'. If in any doubt, hold the dog on top for as long as possible. If they are fully locked, there is no reason why he cannot be turned round in the back to back tie position. Once the dog has mated he should be rested and not tried again for at least a further day.

I cannot stress too strongly that you must always remain calm and patient – you might feel really irritated at his stupidity but do not let him know it. Keep praising him, as a lot depends on his confidence for future matings.

ARTIFICIAL INSEMINATION
This method of conception is really not an issue for breeders in the UK, but like all progressive techniques, it obviously has uses in other countries, where blood lines have a much smaller gene pool. Also, some countries are so vast and the travelling so costly that artificial insemination can be a welcome part of dog breeding.

There is no use waiting for the bitch to come in season and then to consider artificial insemination, you have to obtain permission from the Kennel Club and the Ministry of the country concerned. This will need to be started a long while before the semen is needed. Although it is not a difficult job to obtain the semen from the dog, it is not so easy to inseminate the bitch and veterinary expertise is called for. Fresh semen can be used immediately but the more common use would be for frozen semen. Once frozen, the semen can last for years and no doubt has proved invaluable in breeds with a limited gene pool.

I have a feeling that most breeders in the UK would not allow their dog to submit to artificial insemination but we must realise that there is a genuine need in some countries.

THE IN-WHELP BITCH
Once mated, your bitch will continue in season, and do not think that if conception has taken place the season will finish quicker. Over the years I have found no hard evidence to support this. The season will last for a further week at least; check her carefully before she

goes back with the family. The vulva will decrease in size and appear darker, almost greyish. She will lose that flirtatiousness, and if the other dogs sniff at her, they will probably be told off. If the other dogs go crazy after her and she seems embarrassed by the attention, take no chances and keep her in 'purdah' for a few more days. You will probably notice no difference in her immediate behaviour, but the observant owner will see that about 20 to 30 days after mating, she may become somewhat fussy over her food. If she will not eat her normal food, I do believe in pandering to her whims and tempting her with some favourites. Other than keeping an eye on her, she is best left to a perfectly normal life, and there is no need to feed extra food if her diet is good – the addition of any supplements could make her food less attractive.

Apart from these few days around the third week after mating, no other specific signs are noticeable. Then around the sixth week, you should see a widening of her girth and her teats may start looking pink and tender. By the seventh week, she should show a dip in her underbelly line, her teats will be supple, enlarged and decidedly pinkish, and if you examine the vulva, this will be soft and rather pliable. At the eighth week there is often a change of shape, where the load seems to shift and the belly changes from round to dropped in appearance. The load seems to appear narrower, yet heavier, with a definite sunken look at the top, so that the abdomen appears pear-shaped. This means that nature is preparing for the birth, and I often find that the bitch can become quite quiet a few days prior to whelping. However, this is by no means the rule. One of my own bitches was playing happily with the others, and it was sheer luck that I noticed her turning to look at her stomach, and thinking she had better rest I brought her in to her whelping room, where within half an hour she produced the

The teats of a pregnant bitch may appear pink and tender.
Photo: Haslett.

By the seventh week, there will be a dip in her underbelly line.   *Photo: Haslett.*

first of eight puppies! Do not be caught out, she should not be left unattended with the other dogs for five days prior to her due date.

During her pregnancy she should have remained happy and healthy. If you should see any sign of colour discharge, you should be concerned. It is perfectly possible that she will continue with a dark crimson discharge, and while this should be investigated it does not mean that she is miscarrying. I have seen examples of a bitch showing just such a discharge, and despite all the doom and gloom-merchants predicting this as a miscarriage, the bitch in question went on to full-term, producing six large healthy babies. My own feeling about this is that she actually conceived many more babies than the womb was capable of holding and this was nature's way of getting rid of the surplus. However, all discharges should be looked at by a veterinary

surgeon, and an injection of antibiotic might be helpful.

Should a discharge appear at a later stage, perhaps green or dark red in colour, then you urgently need assistance as this is a very different scenario, and often indicates a dead puppy or the start of infection.

PREPARING FOR WHELPING
You will need to decide where your bitch is to whelp, and it is very important that she is introduced to her new whelping quarters long before the big day. If she is to whelp indoors, or in some room she is not used to, start feeding her there as soon as she is over her season so she will get used to this new environment and associate it with pleasurable things. There is a real danger in moving the in-whelp bitch to strange surroundings, and if she is not totally happy with the set-up then it is best to pander to her whims.

Having ascertained that she must be perfectly at home in her whelping quarters, we must talk about what she is going to have as a bed. It is a nice thought that she can have a box with a top and three sides, but remember that even though she will feel secure and cosy, you will have difficulty in seeing what is happening. A box with a hinged top will be ideal, and if it has a fold-down front, then so much the better. If you have a handyman to make a box in wood then that is excellent, or you can buy a readymade box of rigid PVC.

Shelties vary in size but a typical whelping box for the average Sheltie would be 25 ins high, 25 ins wide and 30 ins deep, with the folded front 12 ins high. and I must say that when one of my bitches is heavily in whelp it does seem rather too high a jump, and I might well resort to a box with a completely detachable front. The PVC is very easy to clean and even after some years' use it is spotless. Wooden boxes look nice painted white, but you must take great care to scrub it thoroughly and even repaint it between uses. I always put a thick layer of newspaper in the box, and while it might not look very superior, at least these can be removed and replaced frequently. Before whelping time I find that bitches like a soft fleecy blanket to lie on, though for the actual whelping the newspapers are sufficient and save a lot of washing.

As her time gets closer, the bitch will often start 'nesting' by ripping the newspapers to shreds. This may make it more comfortable for her, and it is nature's way of not only giving her some project to attend to but also of ensuring a ready nest for the babies. Usually this nesting is not started until she feels time is getting close, but this is not necessarily so, and I have known a bitch to dig in her bed from as early as the halfway stage.

People often ask me how they can tell when a bitch is starting to come into labour, and I must admit that I wish I knew the answer! It would have saved me many a sleepless night. My rule is that they cannot whelp more than five days early or five days late of the due date for a successful litter. You must be observant, and while not allowing yourself to become paranoid, you must watch for those little telltale signs. If your bitch is young and having her first litter, you can expect her to whelp more suddenly than an older bitch, where the muscles have become more flaccid. The state of pre-labour, or stage one, is very hard to spot. She may look round at her stomach, as if wondering why that burning feeling will not go away; she may also become clinging and want to stay near you. The refusal of food is a sure sign, though a greedy bitch might well eat, and be sick once the contractions start. During this first stage she must not be treated like an invalid, and no doubt will benefit from supervised exercise. Take her temperature – the normal is about 101.5F, and anything lower than this means that the birth is getting close. The temperature can go as low as 99.5F and this definitely means that the puppies are on their way. I must admit that I almost never take the temperature, and I have never missed a delivery yet – if you and your bitch are friends, you will know when she is getting uncomfortable. Make sure that her rear is clean – I keep the hair round the vulva clipped away as there is often a mucus discharge which will mat up if left.

10 WHELPING AND REARING

So, your observance has paid off, and you are now sure that your bitch is progressing into stage two – the actual labour.

WHELPING

With a young bitch, the onset of labour can be almost instant and can easily catch you out. She should feel totally secure and at home in her whelping box, running into her home quite happily. If you are having to persuade her to go in, she does not like it, and my advice would be not to get too heavy-handed, but to go along with her choice of where to deliver the first puppy, as you can always move her and the baby. Usually, once the first puppy has arrived, she will be so busy cleaning it that she will happily stay in her proper whelping box.

She will probably start panting, looking round at her rear, and begin frantically digging in her bed. Observe closely, as she will begin contractions. This is a heaving motion along her back, and it is important that you try to note the time of the first contraction. A second strain might follow on, until the straining becomes rhythmic and possibly accompanied by a deep groan. You might hear a flood of fluid being released – this is the water sac, which acts as a lubricant and usually means that the head of the first puppy is not far behind. The bitch will lick and clean herself, but still the contractions come. If you feel either side of the rectum with your thumb and forefinger you will be able to feel a hard lump, and this is the puppy being projected into the birth canal. Her straining will come much more frequently now, and a few gentle words from you will be very welcome, but do not be so concerned that you get in the way of her concentration.

The lump will now be obvious, and the area between rectum and vulva will look swollen. Another push, and the tip of the nose will show, covered in its sac.

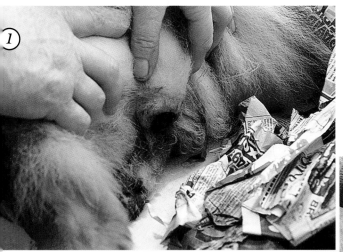

WHELPING
Photos: Haslett.

1. Feel either side of the retum for the imminent birth.

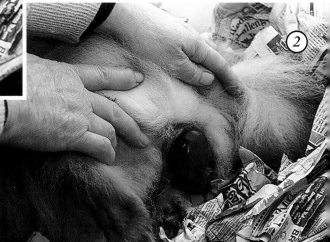

2. The water sac will precede the birth.

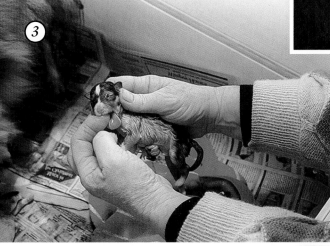

3. The puppy's face must be cleared immediately.

4. The newborn puppy is placed on one side so that it does not get wet.

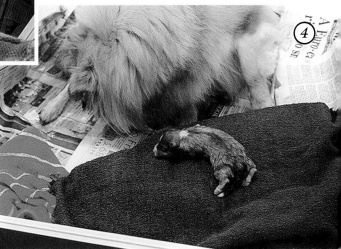

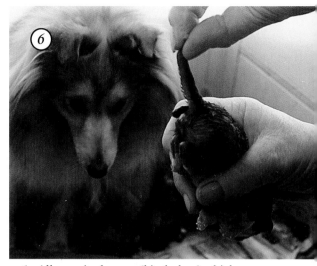

5. Always check that the tongue is not stuck to the roof of the mouth.

6. All puppies have a 'birthplug' which the mother removes.

A maiden bitch might give a sharp cry at the next contraction, and in fact she may even leap up in panic. Try to reassure her and lay her down again, although the final delivery may well take place with her standing in a crouch position. This makes things harder for you, as you will have to feel for the head of the puppy instead of being able to see the presentation. The shoulders should then follow and the hard part is over for the new mother, and as you hold the head and shoulders with a clean towel the rest of the body slithers out.

It is very important to clear the face of the puppy immediately. The new mother will be eagerly licking at the warm damp bundle that has just arrived, which will stimulate breathing, and having ascertained that the head is clear of the sac, give the puppy a vigorous rub to make sure that he is breathing. Then, you can check the umbilical cord – it is usual for the afterbirth (placenta) to be on a longish membrane and to follow on once the puppy has arrived, although the whole lot can swoosh out with that final push. If that happens, then the umbilical must be severed. It is very important that the afterbirth comes away with each puppy, and on absolutely no account should the umbilical be severed until the placenta has followed. A retained afterbirth can hold up subsequent deliveries and if not discharged, will inevitably cause infection. It can be nerve-racking if a puppy is delivered, but still held close to the vulva, but do not pull on the puppy in an effort to free the afterbirth. Gently feel as far along the umbilical as you can and ease it very gently. If it will not come, do not panic, speak reassuringly and wait a few moments before trying to ease the umbilical down again. To pull too harshly could result in one of two disasters – either severing of the cord, leaving the afterbirth inside, or triggering a heavy bleeding, as the placenta adheres closely against the wall of the womb. The little whelp will come to no harm as long as the face is clear and he is breathing. Patience and a steady hand are needed.

Your bitch's natural instinct is to eat the placenta and chew through the cord, so you must be quick to beat her to it. About three inches from the puppy's stomach, press hard with the thumb and forefinger of one hand, and with the thumb and forefinger of your other hand, shred the cord with your nails. Yes, it looks so much more professional to do this with artery forceps and scissors, but thumb and forefinger are so much quicker, so much less stressful for the new mother, and I have never, ever had an umbilical bleed. Your bitch will check that you have done the job properly, and you can scoop the placenta into your waste bag.

I like to offer my new mother a reward for her hard work and give her a drink of evaporated milk, well diluted with boiled water and offered warm. If she is too busy, a little spot put on her nose with your finger will usually start her lapping. It is thirsty work, but do

Sheltie puppies vary in weight. This pup tips the scales at 8.5oz.

not allow her too much. If she refuses to drink, then perhaps puppy number two is on the way. With a maiden bitch the births can follow immediately, whereas a mature bitch can go for quite a long while between deliveries. Follow the same procedure.

Sometimes the new infant goes straight to the 'milk-bar' and this seems to pacify the mother. Once she starts heavy contractions for the next whelp, you could remove the first one to the side as he may get a drenching. However, you must use your common sense as your bitch may not tolerate the absence of her puppy, and so by trying to do the right thing you may cause her stress. If this is so, then her wishes are paramount. While she is delivering the second whelp, I take the opportunity to weigh the first puppy. Sheltie puppies vary enormously, but I would suggest that about six to eight ounces is the average birth weight. When you have him on the scales, check that he is drying nicely and that there are no hind dewclaws.

While your bitch was pregnant you will have guessed at the number of puppies being carried. It is possible, if the puppies are large and healthy, that you have overestimated, or it could be that the puppies are small and puny, and you may be in for a larger number than you were expecting. In either case it is very difficult to know when the last puppy has been born. The usual gentle palpating of the stomach will reveal a lump, but whether this is the now-empty womb knotting up or the final puppy can sometimes be a question of luck! My advice is to stay and watch for any telltale signs.

AFTER WHELPING

The mother should be happily and busily cleaning her puppies and herself. As well as that warm, well-diluted drink of evaporated milk offered after each puppy, and assuming they are all safely arrived, I find that the mother will relish a small meal. Take two eggs, beat them, add nothing (no milk, no butter) and cook them until set, in a microwave if you have one, otherwise in a non-stick pan. Feed warm, not hot, and I am

sure she will appreciate this. If she totally refuses, then do not pester her but take the dish away, sit and wait. Could there be a late addition? You can always warm the eggs up and present them to her at a later time.

Do not be in a hurry to clean up, it will cause stress to the new mother to have her papers scooped out – they smell familiar. Caution must be taken not to upset her. Try to be as certain as you can that there are no more whelps to surprise you before you take her out to relieve herself. It is useless to put her outdoors while you clean up, as the good attentive mother will stay right by the door and will not urinate. I like to lift my new mother out of the bed, giving lots of praise, and take her outdoors just quickly enough to relieve herself before she races back to her litter. You can then clean up, with a sponge and warm water wipe one half of the box, place your clean fleecy bedding down and lift the puppies onto it, she will soon join them. You can then quickly wipe down the other half of the box and pull the bedding under her. Check that all the puppies are feeding, you may well need to encourage any smaller ones. Continuously reassure the mother and if one of the puppies does not seem able to nurse, you will have to open its mouth and clamp it onto a teat, hold it on, and with your other hand gently express some of the mother's colostrum. Keep a careful eye on this puppy. There can be few more rewarding sights than a proud mother with a healthy litter and you have the satisfaction of knowing that you have done your best.

PROBLEMS DURING WHELPING

One of the nightmares a breeder can face is a problem during the whelping. Luckily for us, Shelties are a natural breed and usually give birth with the minimum of effort. I always stay with my bitches during the whelping, though it was often thought unnecessary and many of the older breeders frowned on me for being fussy! You can be too invasive, but I think the bitches find their owner's presence reassuring – and should things not go according to plan then you are on hand.

TIGHT OR BREECH BIRTHS

Sometimes a head will appear in the entrance of the vulva, but despite constant contractions it will not progress. With a piece of clean towelling, grip the head firmly. It is surprising how you will be able to ease the shoulders through, but do not pull hard and do not pull if the bitch is not straining. Applying a gentle, firm pressure, try easing first one side then the other. If you have some petroleum jelly to smear round the extended skin of the vulva, then so much the better. The bitch can understandably get very fretful at a time like this, and you may need to restrain her head – there is no

point in getting bitten, as she may panic and try to bite at the cause of the pain.

If you see a hind foot appear, do not panic. I have thought that breech births account for a quarter of all deliveries. However, it is important that the delivery does not take too long, as once the protective sac is broken the whelp's instinct is to start breathing. Again, your towel is needed, and with a firm grip on the one foot, try to feel where the other foot is, as once both feet are presented you must pull the puppy clear. If the bitch is straining then coincide a gentle but firm pull with each contraction. It is important to bring this puppy into the world as he will be swallowing fluid. Again, the bitch will probably react to the shoulders and head coming through. Once the puppy has arrived, you must immediately clear the head, open his mouth, make sure that the tongue is not stuck to the roof of the mouth, and with your one finger in the side of his mouth, your thumb and other forefinger gripping his head, shake him downwards two or three times to clear his airways. Once you are sure that he has started gasping, then attend to the umbilical and, telling the mother what a clever girl she is, let her tumble him around with her tongue to stimulate him. If fluid gets in the lungs, it will turn to pneumonia, and in a day or two you will have a very poorly puppy – in fact, the puppy that has swallowed fluid might well develop a 'cold' and have the snuffles. Keep a careful eye on him, as at best you will have to keep his nose wiped, but at worst he will run a temperature and will need antibiotic.

INERTIA

One of the most alarming things that can happen is uterine inertia. It can take many forms, and it is hard to be certain if the bitch has become inert. One cause can be that she has conceived only one or two puppies, and they are high up and not causing the muscle contractions to start. If the waters break and nothing further happens, I suggest a trip to the vet for an injection to try to start contractions. How long to wait after that heavy loss of fluid? I would say between two and four hours, or you run the risk of losing your puppies. Another cause of inertia is that the bitch is very heavily in whelp, and the puppies carried too low to engage and start the birth process. In this case, I try a vigorous run around in order to shift the load into a presentable position. The waters may well break, and the bitch just sit there looking sorry for herself. Under these circumstances veterinary attention is essential. I see no reason to inject her to try to start the contractions on this occasion, as it may only give her a belly-ache with no result. A Caesarean section is called for, and this is not the worry it once was. Modern anaesthetics mean that there is no reason why you should not be presented with a live litter, and unless there were problems

with the anaesthetic, the bitch should be able to start feeding the puppies herself. In the case of a large litter, why not start feeding them a supplementary feed yourself? It takes nerve if you have not hand-fed before, but it is so rewarding, and will relieve the mother until she begins feeling better.

Yet another cause of inertia is poor kennel management. The bitch must be quite happy with her environment; she should not be stressed. I said earlier that it is unwise to move her immediately prior to the whelping, she should feel quite relaxed and confident, having had weeks prior to the big day to become accustomed to her whelping quarters. Although she will welcome you as her owner, staying quietly with her, she will not appreciate the whole family coming in to share her big moment, and if there are other dogs in close proximity they may possibly be making her feel inhibited. It is worth putting a lot of thought into the whole thing, but having said that, remember that giving birth is a perfectly natural function and you must not adopt the attitude of being over fussy, making her feel an invalid.

STREPTOCOCCAL INFECTION

Shelties do seem prone to uterine infections and one often hears of puppies being born underweight and puny, even to a fading litter. Once again there are lessons to be learned. If the bitch begins whelping in the normal fashion, presenting a tiny puppy, you should treat its arrival in the usual manner – drying it, removing the umbilical and determining that the airways are clear. Try to get the puppy to feed from the mother, as this first colostrum contains vital antibodies and even if you have to hand-feed throughout, it will act as an insurance if some of this first valuable milk can be swallowed by the puppy. It is worth trying to fasten him onto a teat, but the chances are slim that he will be able to get the full suction necessary, so hold him on and gently work the soft flesh round the nipple for him. After this, bottle feeding is essential if he is to be saved.

Anyone who has bred Shelties for a while will, in all likelihood, have come up against a streptococcal infection. A perfectly normal and healthy bitch can produce puppies that are puny and these will often die. It seems to me that there are two forms of Beta Haemolytic Streptococcal (BHS) – the first, where the puppies are skeletal and underdeveloped, and without hand-feeding these will die. The other form is the birth of a healthy-looking litter which begins feeding, but which becomes languid and limp by the second day. These puppies can be seen to nurse from their mother, and therefore no doubt ingesting a double dose of the BHS infection. Both forms of BHS are heartbreaking and treatment must be administered before you

attempt to breed from the bitch again. It will not go away on its own.

Assuming that you have had a litter where the puppies are born tiny, they will appear premature, with all their ribs showing, tails like pieces of string, and with a strawberry redness about them. Amazingly they are often quite vigorous and it is perfectly possible to save them. The first and vital thing to do is to feed them. If you wrap them up and take them to the vet you are losing valuable time, much better to employ your time by making up a syringe and feeding the puppies yourself. I have a criterion that any puppy under four ounces requires a feed on arrival. Try to get it to ingest some colostrum, as the chances are that it may well find its way to the breast but will be too weak to suck. After the first feed, then you can seek veterinary help, as an antibiotic injection will help the puppy fight the infection, but I cannot stress too strongly that it is your feeding that will save his life. With weak puppies, this must be carried out at least every two hours. Now, any new mother becomes stressed by her puppies being lifted out of the bed, so it is necessary to prepare the feed, carry it to her, plus hot water to keep it all at blood temperature, and then, kneeling down in front of the whelping box, feed the newborn puppy right there in front of the mother. It will be prudent to talk sweet words to reassure her!

Should the puppies be born a good weight, but become flaccid a few hours later, then it could be the fading puppy syndrome. If they are not feeding, the tummy will feel hollow, and once again feeding every two hours is the only hope of saving them – plus an antibiotic injection.

It could be argued that the fading puppy form of BHS is the hardest to combat. It might be better to remove the puppies from the mother if they are feeding, as it is her milk which is carrying the infection. However; think hard, because hand rearing is an exhausting job and must be done every two hours, and involves not only feeding the puppies, but doing the bitch's job of cleaning all orifices with moist cotton wool. There are several variants of BHS, and it is not possible to know beforehand if your bitch has contracted it, but she must be swabbed and treated with antibiotics after the first disaster. It might be prudent to re-test her during the season when you next intend breeding. BHS can be caught at the time of mating, or during the bitch's season, when the lips of the vulva are enlarged, and urinating is frequent. One naturally thinks that hygiene must play a part.

CARE OF THE NEW MOTHER

After your bitch has had her puppies, the bed is cleaned out, she has been

A contented litter all feeding from their mother.

taken out, probably under protest at leaving her babies, and given her scrambled egg, she should be left to rest. It is worth keeping an eye on the whelping box as you may have misjudged the number of puppies due! It is usually at this stage that I go and shower and change my own clothes and take a well-earned cup of coffee back to the nursery and just sit in front of the new mother, taking stock of the situation. If the puppies are feeding well, their tongues show round the teat and they are silent. By the next day, they should have mastered the art of sucking so well that their heads will jerk back and forth, their tails raised in ecstasy, while mother snoozes happily. The first couple of days are quiet, the mother enjoying four light meals only. I continue with the scrambled egg for one meal, and for the second meal she will enjoy some good quality chopped beef fed raw. The two intermittent meals are well-diluted evaporated milk.

Place her feed bowl between her front legs and start off with a little placed on her nose – this usually will get her eating or lapping. If she has not eaten the placentas she should keep a steady stomach. However, if the afterbirths have been eaten then she will almost certainly have diarrhoea, often black in colour. This is nothing to worry about, but she will feel a lot better once the stool firms up. It is perfectly normal for her to have a vaginal discharge, in fact this is part of the cleansing process. Just

When the puppies are four months old the mother will be completely out of coat. Photo: Haslett.

check that it is not excessive, turning green in colour or smelling offensive. If any of these three things occur, she must be taken to the vet for antibiotics.

On the third day after the whelping, the gentle flow of colostrum will increase to a full flow of milk and the breasts may well become hardened. Encourage the puppies to feed from all the teats; sometimes the last two pairs of teats become really hard. This can develop into mastitis if left unchecked. I suggest gently expressing some of the milk and rubbing a little baby oil into the breast to keep it soft and supple. If left to become mastitis, it can cause, at best, heavy discomfort to the mother, and fever and milk retention at worst. Should the latter state develop, a course of antibiotics is essential. The mother's appetite will increase – continue the four meals each day, increasing the amount daily. There is no reason why she should lose weight during the whole nursing period; just increase her rations, particularly meat. If she has plenty of high protein food and diluted milk drinks, she should stay happy and content.

There is a condition called eclampsia which can occur when the calcium level falls dangerously low in the bitch's body. The observant owner will have noticed a staring look in her eyes and an unsteadiness when she walks. If not treated this will progress to a heavy panting and a fading into unconsciousness, which could be fatal – a trip to the vet for a calcium injection will show immediate results.

By the end of the first week she should be eating well, enjoying short trips in the garden, and happily looking after her family. By the end of the second week she will leave the puppies for longer periods, and it is during this stage that I like to give the mother a bath, she will feel so much fresher and enjoy the attention. Care must be taken to keep her nails short as she will not have been exercising as normal to wear them down. Feed her well, as her milk is being produced in abundance at this stage. During the next week your first attempts to feed the puppies will start which will ease the burden.

By the end of the third week she should be able to 'escape' from the selfish attentions of her family – perhaps a break of a couple of hours in the morning and again in the afternoon. By the end of the fourth week she can leave them for her morning break as before and in the afternoon it would be wise for her to leave them until bedtime.

By the end of the fifth week she will be ready to sleep elsewhere, just paying daytime visits to the brood to check that our kennel management is as good as hers! It is about this time that I like to give the mother a further bath, a worming, express her anal glands and, of course, check those nails. She can now rejoin the rest of the dogs for walks in the fields, though those visits to her puppies are much enjoyed. She will be losing a little coat, especially on her belly-line, but otherwise she should be looking good. The heavy coat loss will not start until the puppies reach about ten weeks and then she will cast her coat like never before – it is no use brushing, as your brush will be clogged straight-away. I resort to that invaluable wide-toothed comb and, every day, rake out as much of the old coat as I can. She will eventually look like a smooth version of our lovely breed. I always think they look so adorable at this stage, more like a gangly puppy. The coat will be at its most sparse when the pups are four to five months old, and then new coat growth comes, all fresh and rich in colour. She will not be back in full bloom until her puppies are six months old, and even then she will not complete the full feathering until they are seven to eight months old.

HAND-REARING

To hand-rear a healthy puppy is a whole lot easier than hand-rearing a 'tiny' who is combating infection as well as almost starving. It is a matter of life and death – your most valuable asset is an alarm clock, as the puppies must be fed every two hours. The mixture I have used for years with great success is evaporated milk, boiling water and glucose or sugar. Pour one tablespoon of evaporated milk, add exactly the same amount of boiling water, add a pinch of sugar (or a level teaspoon of glucose powder, if you have it), mix, and when at room temperature, draw two ccs into a small syringe that has been placed in boiling water to sterilise it prior to use. Kneeling in front of the new mother, find the puppy that is to be fed, open his mouth, and make sure that the tongue is not stuck to the roof of the mouth. Push the syringe into the mouth and very, very gently depress the plunger. You will have to hold the head of the puppy steady with the syringe in place with one hand, while you depress the plunger with the other. It is absolutely imperative that the feeding is done gently, as the syringe will squirt the liquid otherwise, and the puppy's lungs will almost certainly get some of the mixture in them, with the end result of pneumonia setting in.

Even the weakest of puppies usually shows a reaction to food. If the puppy swallows on his own, then take heart as he may progress. If he lies with the mixture trickling out of the side of his mouth then I would say that his chances of survival are slim.

Having given the first feed, you must check the time and set that alarm clock for two hours ahead – day or night, this feeding must be accomplished. If you are feeding only one poorly puppy, it is easier than coping with a whole litter. If you are feeding more than one, it is important that the milk mixture is kept warm, so take a bowl of hot water to the 'nursery' so that the bowl or cup containing the mixture is warmed for each syringe.

As long as the mother is reassured, she will accept your caring for her puppy. If you take the puppy out of her bed, her instinct will be to leap up after it, so it is much better to kneel in front of the bed. She will get to enjoy the attention and cleaning the mouths of the hand-fed puppies.

You will be able to assess if you are winning – the puppies fill out remarkably quickly. After the third or fourth feed, the scrawny stomachs should at least have filled and as long as you persevere you stand a good chance of saving a life. People often tell me that they are afraid of overfeeding – my usual fear is underfeeding. If you miss a feed, then there is a real danger of the puppy developing colic when fed again,

119

as air will invade the stomach. Remember, if you are feeding more than one, that each puppy is an individual, and one may need slightly less than two ccs, while the next one needs four ccs.

After a day or two, you will hopefully see that the puppies are trying to suck on the syringe and it might be possible to progress to a premature baby's feeding bottle. Make sure that milk can come out of the nipple, as the suck of the little puppy is feeble compared to that of a human baby. It might even be necessary to increase the size of the holes, which you can do with a hot needle. Be careful not to let air get into the puppy; the bottle must be held up so that the nipple points down. Never lower the end of the bottle or air will be sucked in.

Having recommended my evaporated milk method for hand-rearing puppies,

I have also recently tried a commercial milk replacer, with which I have had excellent results. Remember, Shelties do not do well on too much cereal, and I am suspicious of many of the rearing milks on the market – they are probably fine for some other breed, but for Shelties I would recommend either the evaporated milk method, or a quality milk replacer. Make sure you follow follow the manufacturer's mixing instructions. It would be sheer folly to change the puppies' mixture, so whatever you start with, stay with it.

Warmth has to be increased for hand-reared puppies. I would suggest that the whelping box should be at a constant 75F and, obviously, draught-free. With a litter that are already coping with stress and fighting infection, I would increase the heat for the first few days, maybe even to 80F. However, the mother must be comfortable and

For the first couple of weeks, the puppies will divide their time between eating and sleeping. Photo: Carol Ann Johnson.

nothing will be achieved if she is constantly leaving the bed to cool off!

TUBE-FEEDING

If you prefer, the weakling can be tube-fed. Tube and syringe kits can be bought at a veterinary surgery. This method is not for the faint hearted. You will need to measure the tube carefully, hold one end of the tube to the puppy's nose, and literally stretch puppy and tube together, marking the point that is level with the furthest rib with either nail varnish or some waterproof plaster, this is the length of tube that will be inserted into the mouth. There is a definite knack to it – get it wrong and the puppy will die.

Dip the end of the tube into the mixture, open the puppy's mouth and quickly insert the tube. He may swallow as it touches his throat; feed the tube on down the throat until the mark you have made is level with the mouth, then put your ear to the tube end and listen – you should be able to hear him breathe. Taking courage in both hands, fix the syringe with the required amount of mixture to the end of the tube and gently depress the plunger. Tube feeding is much quicker and, as the puppies use no energy during the feed, they grow well. However, if you have never tube-fed before, you must get someone to show you and you must be very careful – one mistake and the food will be in the lung, with disastrous results.

REARING YOUR SHELTIE PUPPIES

If everything has gone well, the first three weeks should be easy for you with the new mother doing all the work.

DEWCLAWS

If you found hind dewclaws on the puppies, then these need removing at four to five days old. In the UK the front dewclaws are not removed – it is felt that, being a natural working breed, the less 'doctoring' done, the better. If hind dewclaws are found, then armed with a sharp pair of scissors that have been previously sterilised, a wad of cotton-wool and a small tub of silver nitrate, I tackle the job. If you have someone who will take the mother outside to keep her occupied while this job is done, then so much the better.

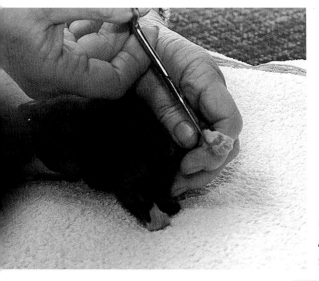

Occasionally a puppy will have hind dewclaws which will need to be removed.

Assess the shape of the dewclaw. Some are fat and cling to the foot, and these are the ones that might bleed; the loose, flexible type are easy to remove. Wipe the area with moist cotton-wool and then deftly put the scissor blade either side of the whole joint; check the angle is close to the foot, and cut. If done quickly the puppy might start, but will seldom cry. Press dry cotton-wool on the wound and wait. Should the wound bleed, then put a pinch of silver nitrate on it and attend to the other dewclaw, although I have had occasions when only one hind foot has a dewclaw. This little job done, it is time for the mother to come back in and she will immediately know something is amiss –

reassure her and try giving her a favourite meal to keep her occupied. The nails of the puppies will need to be kept short as there is no point in having mothers' breasts scratched. I usually keep a pair of sharp nail scissors near the whelping bed so the puppies nails are cut frequently – at least once a week.

EARLY SOCIALISATION

When the puppies are about 12 days old their eyes begin to open – you will notice if you hold them up to the light a little chink reflecting back at you. It is an exciting time and well worth your observation, as occasionally an eye can be slow to open, in which case I would apply a little Vaseline on the rims and in

Weaning can be a messy business, but it does not take long for the puppies to get the idea.

a day or two try to ease the rims apart. It is possible that they have become stuck with matter. Always be gentle. The eyes are not focusing at this stage, and the ears will start to hear because they too have been previously closed. So that helpless little puppy is soon able to take stock of the world and whereas they just lay contentedly, they will begin reacting to sounds. I always have a radio playing in the nursery, and believe in chatting to get them used to the sound of human voices.

It is absolutely vital that these puppies are handled – I have a cushion that is placed in front of the whelping box where I sit and waste my time! At first the puppies are lifted out one by one and placed on my lap, where we get to know each other and I can check on nail cutting, eye examinations, coats and any other little point. It is not long before they are staggering out to pull my shoelaces and play with the toys provided.

REGISTRATION

It is usually at this stage that I think about registering the litter with the national Kennel Club. This completes the process of registering the puppies that was started at the time of mating. For established procedures, contact your national Kennel Club for advice. Hopefully these registrations will be processed in time for you to hand over with the pedigree and diet sheet to the new owners.

FEEDING

The average size of a litter for Shelties is four. I have had a variance on this from a singleton to eleven! Should there be a large number of puppies it would be wise to start feeding early. I have started puppies off on solid food as young as 12 days old, so I know that they can take it.

Assuming that you have four healthy puppies, at three weeks introduce them to their first feed. Nowadays there are really marvellous puppy weaning foods on the market. Like all old fashioned breeders I used to start off with raw chopped beef, but now I mix a little of the wonderful puppy weaning porridge readily available. Food is more palatable when warm, so putting a little in a shallow dish, I offer them their first feed. Do not be disappointed if it is not appreciated. They may be getting so much from their mother and cannot face anything else – persevere, and offer a meal later on, or the next day. You will probably have to guide their heads to the dish at first, and restrain the one who wants to put both front feet into your cleanly prepared food. By the next day you can introduce some puppy food, either canned or one of the dried forms; if you use the latter, it will need soaking and mashing. A puppy's stomach is small at this age, so 'little and often' is the order of the day. Personally, I prefer not to give milk as not all Shelties can tolerate it, but feeding alternately – puppy weaning porridge and then a solid meal – the puppies should progress onto five to six meals a day by the time they are five weeks old.

If the number of puppies in your litter was only one or two, then the mother can continue sleeping with them. Usually at five weeks of age the puppies can do without mother, and in fact I would put them to bed with an extra meal. It is important for fresh clean water to be accessible at all times – try to buy a water bowl that cannot be tipped over. Although mother does not sleep with her babies at this stage, she should have lots of access, as her breasts will still fill up and the puppies will still benefit from the mother's milk. Mother's presence is invaluable as a play stimulant and for maternal discipline too.

INTRODUCING THE CAR

At six weeks of age my puppies experience a strange thing – their first trip in a car. I can almost hear readers expressing shock horror at this – taking unvaccinated puppies out! It is a tried and tested method! If you have a friend or partner, get them to drive while you cover your lap with a large towel and two puppies are placed on this as you sit in the front seat. Start the engine but do nothing! Just sit and chat as if this is the most normal thing in the world. Perhaps a short journey to the local shop or wherever, and then return home, reward with a small tidbit and

then return them to the others. If you have a large litter, this means several trips as the first introduction to the car must be on your lap. My puppies are seldom, if ever, travel-sick and this early training must be beneficial. I have even put puppies in the car when cleaning it. I might even feed them a meal in the car, so that they associate it with pleasure.

WORMING

The puppies will need worming. It is best to have a worming programme to follow – my own puppies are wormed with a gentle syrup at three and a half weeks, then at five weeks and seven weeks. These wormings are as much precautionary as necessary. A lot has been written in our press about worms and the danger to children of contracting Toxocara Canis, and it would be irresponsible to sell puppies without first worming them. I have not seen a worm for years but still feel it necessary to follow a worming programme.

NEW HOMES

At around seven to eight weeks of age, puppies which are to be sold as pets can leave for their new homes. It is one of the hardest decisions for you to make – which one is your possible future champion? The simple answer is to 'run on' the questionable ones for a later selection, and in the meantime, the ones you are sure are pet quality can be collected. Obviously, recognised breeders receive a number of enquiries, and if you have no puppies of your own then you can recommend a fellow breeder. There is a good feeling of comradeship between breeders. So, how do you set about selling your puppies if it happens to be your first litter?

The owners of the stud dog will probably want to see the puppies, so mention your surplus as they may have some enquiries. Alternatively, an advertisement in the weekly dog papers might bring results, or you could try the 'pets' column in your local paper.

However, when you advertise them remember that these are your babies that you loved and fostered – they deserve a loving permanent home. Even a lovely breed like the Sheltie has Sheltie Rescue added to the various breed clubs. All breeders, whether large or small, owe it to their puppies to follow up with help and advice and the promise to take the dog back in the face of an unexpected disaster.

When your first client is due to look at the puppies, be ready to receive them and make your meeting pleasant. The puppies look good because you have

An outdoor playpen is a great asset when rearing a litter.

paid attention to grooming them and keeping those nails short. You will have assessed the characters of the puppies, so it might be helpful to the prospective owner to mention any little characteristics.

There are a few times when I have refused to sell – you are perfectly within your rights to refuse a sale if you are not satisfied with the prospective owners. Perhaps the children are beyond control and you fear for the safety of your puppy; whatever the reason, you owe it to the puppy to be completely satisfied with the home offered.

Purchase agreed, with both parties happy, you will need to give four pieces of paper when the puppy is handed over – the pedigree, the Kennel Club registration, a diet sheet and a receipt. The pedigree can be of three, four or five generations, and it must be written out carefully. A mistake is often caused by careless handwriting. The registration should have been received from the Kennel Club. There are occasions when this has been delayed,

so you may need to explain with a promise to forward it as soon as it arrives, for this document is the new owner's guarantee of ownership. The diet sheet is absolutely essential – no dog, let alone a puppy, should have a sudden change of diet. You must write down exactly what the puppy has to eat each day, and explain about the increase in rations as the puppy grows. Also, stress that he is not to be exercised too much, and remind them that he should be vaccinated at eight to twelve weeks of age. If a receipt is given, you have the address and can keep in contact to check how the puppy is progressing.

It is sad to see puppies go – they have taken up so much of your time and devotion, but the other way of looking at it is that someone else is going to be as happy as you have been with their mother. You have also made new friends.

Once you have selected your pick of litter you must start as you mean to go on – a lot depends on it.

11 YOUR SHELTIE'S HEALTH

Shelties are a very hardy breed. Our breed Standard used to stress this fact, though sadly it is not a word included today, but like all serious breeders I would suggest that the hardiness along with sturdy frames must be one of our paramount aims. Shelties are easy to keep and perhaps we take this for granted, as I have heard of a few occasions where there has been a kennel fight with the Shelties 'ganging-up' on one member. It would be a very sensible precaution not to kennel too many together if they are to be left unattended. As a breed, Shelties can become very excitable, and one of my own bitches, adorable and gentle as she is at most times, can become very excited at certain sounds. Her agitation takes the place of 'going for' whichever dog is standing next to her – this could lead to a kennel fight, so if my attention is not totally on the dogs, this little lady has a run to herself. It is always better to be safe than sorry!

The Shetland Sheepdog is a hardy breed and should suffer few health problems. Photo: Haslett.

STOOLS

Although it is not common, I am often being told about Shelties with 'dirty trousers'. If this applies to your dog, then you must reconsider his diet. It is only common sense to keep your dog's tummy regular, and no matter what manufacturers may claim, you must try different foods until you find the one which keeps his tummy right. A dog's stool should be dark in colour and solid in appearance. My suggestion would be to increase his protein intake – biscuits can have a laxative effect. Perhaps he has an intolerance to milk, not all dogs can take milk, though the skimmed milk obtainable nowadays seems to solve this problem.

AGEING

The onset of old age is inevitable, but a lot can be done to make the life of an old dog more tolerable. Whilst my 'oldies' love to go for walks, they appreciate returning to a comfortable bed rather than being left outside. There are also many diets for the old dog; personally I believe in spoiling them and continuing with their high-protein diet, and I often make this a more moist feed as, just like humans, their teeth are degenerating. I can well remember a friend telling me her old dog just would not eat and was getting thinner and thinner. When I went to visit and saw a very drastic deterioration in the old dog, I asked to see his food. To my dismay, he was being fed one of those highly-priced hard kibble feeds manufactured specially for the older dog. Common sense must play a vital part in all animal husbandry – and how appreciative the old fellow was when some finely-minced chicken was put

Ch. Lythwood Skymaster (Ch. Sandpiper Of Sharval - Lythwood Snaffy), photographed at 14 years, showing the lasting qualities of the breed. Joint top sire with 12 Champion progeny. Photo: Lund.

down for him in its place, and my advice was to feed frequently, three smaller meals a day, soft and appetising!

ARTHRITIS

To see a dog with arthritis is sad indeed, but there is no need to send him to the happy hunting ground. While I would say that there is really nothing to combat the progression of this disease, here again common sense must prevail – no long vigorous walks, try to eliminate the necessity of him having to climb steps, and do make sure that he has a soft, dry bed in which to relax. I hate to see dogs having shared beds – mine do like a bed of their own, and this prevents the possibility of one 'being polite' and sleeping on the floor, allowing others to have the bed!

Care must be taken to be extra-vigilant with the nails of the arthritic dog – if he has developed an uneven gait, then it is very important that his nails are cut regularly.

BURNS

Burns and scalds should never happen, but if they do, then immediately take the heat out of the affected area by placing an ice-pack rolled in a clean cloth on to it. Sprays specially for burns can be purchased, but accidents usually occur 'out of the blue' and an ice-pack is wonderful for alleviating pain. It might be prudent to cut the hair round the area affected as the skin may blister anyway.

COPRAPHAGIA

This has a horrid meaning – a dog eating his own motions. No one has come up with a definite reason for this. You would think perhaps some vital nutrient is missing from the dog's diet, or maybe he feels his stomach is just not full enough. If you find your dog persisting in this horrible habit, try adding extra iron to his diet, or even some green vegetable, which you will have to cook and mash to disguise its presence among his food. If this has no effect, increase his food rations, or even give an extra meal during the day. It goes without saying that you should pick up all matter as soon as it is dropped, but the dog that develops this habit can become very crafty. You must let him know that this behaviour is not allowed or tolerated. You could perhaps give him an extra 'chew' as a distraction and to keep him occupied, as bad habits often stabilise through boredom.

COUGHS

There is a very virulent infection known as kennel cough. Any dog can contract this – not just a dog living in a kennel. The first signs are a sore throat, and an observant owner will notice the dog constantly swallowing and maybe reacting to the pressure of his collar on the throat. To be truthful, there is very little that can be done once the infection is contracted; some of the cough mixtures made for humans are as good as anything. Within about three days of the start of the sore throat, a short rasping cough will develop. Depending on his reaction to the infection this could progress to a really racking cough, with him trying to clear his throat by standing hunched-up, head lowered, while he coughs and coughs. Change of temperature affects the airways, so try to keep him in a steady environment until he is better.

I need hardly say that once you suspect kennel cough, you should immediately quarantine your dog and not let him mix with others outside his home.

CUTS
If a cut occurs, this must be bathed and any foreign matter picked out. If heavy bleeding occurs this must be quelled by applying a clean swab of cotton-wool or even a tissue, if nothing else is to hand, and pressing hard on the wound. Once the bleeding has ceased, then you can assess the damage. If it is superficial, some antibiotic powder can be sprinkled on the surface of the wound, but if the cut is deeper and flesh is visible, then it will need stitching and a trip to your vet is essential.

DIARRHOEA
This can have several causes, and all need treating, but the main cause is infection. If your Sheltie has a sudden bout of diarrhoea, stop all food and give water only for the rest of the day. To be ultra-safe, boil the water first and watch him closely. It might be a precaution to add some glucose after the first 12 hours. Only after 24 hours should you offer any food – no red meat or dry kibble food; the safest thing to offer is a little finely shredded white meat (chicken breast would be ideal). Make the first meal small – it is much better to offer food 'little and often' than to extend the already delicate stomach. Once he has started eating again you can mix a little arrowroot into the food.

Shelto The Gipsy Princess (Ch. Shelto The Gay Piper – Shelto Fleuraleigh): Note the gleaming coat and excellent condition of this dog.
Photo: D. Moore.

Keep him on a white meat diet until the stool is once again a 'sausage' shape – it will probably take a few days before his motions regain the correct colour and consistency. If your puppies get diarrhoea, then waste no time in seeking veterinary advice, as antibiotics are a life-saver.

However; people so often tell me that their vet recommends boiled rice. Remember that Shelties are not cereal eaters, and they are much better on boiled white meat, as previously mentioned, until the stool is shaped. Then normal food can be gradually reintroduced.

EAR INFECTIONS

With plenty of air able to get into the ear, Shelties are not prone to ear trouble. If your dog starts holding his head on one side or scratching an ear, it is worth investigating. If the inside of the ear looks inflamed or dirty with brown wax, then clean the ear gently with a cotton bud, and when you are satisfied that no grass seed or similar irritant has got into the ear, then one of the proprietary brands of ear drops can be squeezed in. You will probably need to repeat this routine for a few days. It is possible that your Sheltie has contracted ear-mites; these can be caught from cats and must be eradicated. Here again, there are some very efficient products especially made to get rid of these unwelcome pests.

EYE TROUBLES

Sadly, Shelties can be affected by several eye problems. The most common is the unsightly 'runny' eye. There are several causes – the haw or third eyelid could be a tight fit and causing a squeezing of the eyeball, or it could be his tear ducts. It may even be a mere cold in the eye caused by draught.

My usual advice is to do nothing – I have seen a good dog ruined by unnecessary intervention with his tear ducts. Often these runny eyes can be just due to adolescence, and the whole problem will right itself. If the eye persists in watering, the hair will become marked under the eye and it is possible to buy ointment especially made to take tear stains away. Personally I hate to see runny eyes – the whole expression is spoiled, and from a breeder's point of view it is a defect which should be avoided when planning future litters.

FITS

Fits are almost unheard of in our breed. While there is much controversy over the possibility of the occurrence of fits being hereditary, I treat everything as being inherited, and would never under any circumstances whatsoever breed from a dog or bitch that had shown symptoms of having a fit. The symptoms can be an 'absent' look on the dog's face, usually followed by a frothing at the mouth, with the dog shaking and going into full convulsions with a lot of jerking around. If this happens, do not try to release the jaws as they will clamp – in fact the best thing to do is to throw a blanket over the dog so he is in the dark and quiet. He will derive a feeling of safety from this darkened space when he recovers. The length of the seizure will vary and it is quite likely that he will go off in another fit, and veterinary help must be sought. However, urgent help could do little more than the suggested darkened quiet, so instead of getting your vet up out of bed, take your dog along to the next surgery. The chances are that some sedative will be prescribed. I have even heard of a change of diet being recommended, with successful results.

FLEAS AND LICE

I hope that you will never be troubled by either of these! If fleas are present, you will see evidence of horrid black flea dirt, mostly behind the ears or on top of the back. There are some marvellous brands of flea spray available and you should waste no time in spraying your dog liberally. Take stock of his bedding and anywhere else he is likely to lie.

When you have repeated the spraying over a period of several days, give your Sheltie a thorough bath and keep vigilant! Try to eradicate the cause as it might save a lot of discomfort to you both!

Lice are a much harder problem. These are tiny parasites which look a bit like small grains, beige in colour and very contagious. Urgently bath your Sheltie, using several applications of insecticidal shampoo, liberally worked into the skin. Try to comb the worst affected areas with a nit-comb. It would be pointless to put the dog back into the same bed – all bedding must be burnt, any wooden boxes scrubbed with bleach and painted with a wood stain, and as a precaution treat all carpets and skirting boards with which he has been in contact. Puppies heavily infested with lice can become very ill, certainly anaemic, and it is very important to be rid of these horrid little pests.

LAMENESS

With Shelties being the active little dogs they are, it is inevitable that someone will come limping towards you one day! The usual cause is a knock, or rough play. Occasionally stifles can be knocked, though care should be taken that the accident does not recur. If your dog is lame because of a thorn or a grass seed he will usually lick at the sore area, so finding the object is easier than trying to find the problem with a joint. If lameness occurs, curtail the dog's exercise, keep him warm (how useful a cage can be at these times!) and should you suspect stifle damage or a break, then urgent veterinary help is needed. If a bone is broken it is impossible for the dog to put weight on it and it will certainly need attention.

MISMATING

There is no excuse for this, except bad animal husbandry! Should the worst happen then there is no use trying to pull the two apart should you find them 'tied' together. You will have to wait for nature to take its course and then go to the vet for an injection of Stilboestrol. Do not wait to see if she proves to be in whelp, because the chances are that she will be! Once injected the whole cycle of season will be started off again, and you must keep your bitch safe.

MONORCHIDISM

This is a problem in Shelties. Although all male animals have two testicles, it is almost common in our breed, and probably lots of other small breeds, for one or both of the testicles to be retained in the body. Now, all breeders have had experience of this problem, and while we do our best to eradicate it, the problem keeps occurring! However, I do feel that breeders are lenient in allowing so much time for a puppy to become entire. Ideally, a dog puppy should be entire at six weeks of age. To keep a dog on until he is nine months to a year old hoping entirety will develop is, in my opinion, courting trouble, as surely the next generation will also be late in maturing – maybe not even developing at all.

The English Shetland Sheepdog Club used to keep an 'Entire' register, and it is heavily frowned upon to breed from a non-entire dog. A dog with a single testicle is perfectly fertile, whereas one with no testicles cannot reproduce. You would think the problem would therefore be self-eliminating, but this is certainly not the case. Veterinary opinion is that a non-entire male should be operated on and the retained testicle surgically removed; however, my opinion is to leave well alone. The dog will live a perfectly normal life, and I have seldom heard of there being any trouble from a retained testicle – the thought that it might promote a cancer cannot be substantiated. I do hate the thought of surgical intervention if not absolutely necessary.

POISONING

If you suspect any form of poisoning you must seek veterinary help immediately. If your dog refuses food, drinks excessively, or adopts a hunched-up appearance with the stomach feeling tight and tender, then I would urge you to seek advice. Do not attempt to try to make your dog sick as you could be making matters worse. Should you suspect poisoning telephone your vet, keeping the dog warm, as I am a great believer in warmth for all ailments. If the dog should start vomiting, then try to keep the vomit to show the vet what has been brought up. Dogs will often eat grass as a natural way to rid the gut of bile, so do not panic if you see him vomit after eating grass, usually they are bright and cheerful afterwards. The real belly-ache after poisoning is much more severe and the symptoms are much more acute, and it is no use trying a home-made cure without first identifying the poison.

TEETH

Teeth are a law unto themselves – I have had two from the same litter with totally different wear on their teeth. Good teeth are determined at birth – why one puppy from a litter should develop tartar while his sister or brother keeps pearly-white teeth is a mystery. I would love to say that Shelties keep strong teeth into old age, but this is not always the case.

Teeth do need supervision – even in puppies. If baby canine teeth look steadfast even while the adult teeth are developing, they may well need removing by your vet. Without making your puppy wary of having his mouth looked at, try wobbling the baby tooth. If, by five-and-a-half to six months of age, the baby teeth are still firmly in place, it is a wise precaution to get them professionally inspected. In addition to monthly cleaning you should check for disease of the gums; sometimes the gums will recede from the base of the tooth and the tooth will start to decay. I try not to have too much intervention but it is necessary that teeth which are starting to decay are removed. Once decay has set in, there is no use trying to feed hard food as this may cause pain. My Shelties love those chews especially designed for dental care.

TRAVEL SICKNESS

Why some strains of Shelties suffer from travel sickness and others do not is a puzzle. My thoughts are that it is due to temperament. My dogs are all good travellers and puppies leaving home for the first time are all good in the car, so I think it must initially be something inherited. It would seem that here is a matter for confidence-building, and as young as possible I would try putting your puppy in the car, starting the engine and going nowhere! Do not keep fussing him or reassuring him as he will think something awful is about to happen. Just sit quietly, admiring him, and listen to the sound of the engine. After a few minutes reward him with a small tidbit, switch off the engine and return to normal. This could be repeated a few times and he could even have a meal in the car, so hopefully he will not develop a fear at being placed in such a strange environment. Start with short journeys, returning with praise and reward, and eventually become more adventurous by accomplishing longer journeys. You will achieve nothing by putting your puppy in a box and whizzing off to the vet for his first trip in the car. He must learn that nice things are associated with his first journeys to build up his confidence.

Should you be unfortunate enough to have a puppy that is travel sick, then you must act accordingly. Do not leave him at home, but common sense will tell you not to feed him prior to a journey, and be on the ready with absorbent paper towels and a sponge. A dog that salivates excessively uses up a lot of moisture and will need water at the end of the trip. There are lots of travel sickness tablets available; most will make him drowsy, and while I am not decrying their use, I would urge training him to the car before you resort to remedial treatment.

WORMS

All breeders 'worm' their puppies as a matter of kennel management, usually at three, five and seven weeks, so that the new owner should not need to worry over worming again until the puppy is six months of age.

UK owners are lucky in that the only worms of concern are roundworms and tapeworms, and treatment against both of these can be given in the one dose, which is usually repeated in a few days. Roundworms are the most common. Resembling a piece of white string, they can be from two to six inches in length, and if an infestation is present they can form a knot. Usually, evidence is seen in the dog's stool and you must get worm medicine from your vet. Tapeworms are more serious; they can result in loss of condition, and cause the dog to bite at the irritation round his rectum. Evidence can be seen if you examine closely; if you see little beige-coloured segments gather round the rectum, these are a positive indication that tapeworm are present, so you must

obtain a dosage from your vet. Treat not only this dog but any others on the property.

In areas where mosquitoes (the host) proliferate, dogs may be affected by heartworm. Symptoms include coughing, listlessness and intolerance to exercise. Treatment is effective, and is in the form of daily medication during the mosquito season.

HEREDITARY DEFECTS

As science gets more and more clever, it is only natural that defects are found which none of us realised anything about. Like most breeds, Shelties have been found to have a few worries.

There are hereditary conditions concerning the eyes: Collie Eye Anomaly (CEA) is one, and while it does not really affect the sight, if two animals that were badly affected were mated together, there is a possibility of producing a blind puppy. It is for this reason that breeders have tried to eliminate CEA. There is a testing scheme where puppies can be taken as a litter to an eye specialist for screening; then again as an adult to achieve a 'clear' certificate. It is important to keep things in perspective – CEA is non-progressive and no-one would know that your dog's eyes were affected unless they were an eye specialist. Try to view it with common sense as just one part of the dog.

Progressive Retinal Atrophy (PRA) is a different matter and is seldom discovered in Shelties. It cannot be detected until adulthood, so because it is progressive it is viewed with much more concern. If you have the misfortune to have this diagnosed, then obviously, you would not want to perpetuate this by breeding from an affected animal.

Hip Dysplasia (HD): This term is used to describe abnormal hip joints, and affected dogs may suffer minor lameness or be severely incapacitated. There is a scheme where hips can be tested for this condition. It needs an anaesthetic as the hips have to be manipulated and X-rayed. Fortunately for us, Shelties have had very few incidences of HD, as it is more likely to affect medium to large breeds.

12 INFLUENTIAL BRITISH KENNELS

Having compared the differences in the two breed Standards it is worthy of note that the American and British Shelties all have the same origins, so the variations between them can only be man-made! How did it come about that the different points became more desirable on one side of the Atlantic than on the other? It is a puzzle, and I have to say that some of the cream of the early Shelties went out to the USA and they were certainly well-received. Several of the early UK Champions were exported – Ch. Helensdale Laddie from the Helensdale kennels of Mr and Mrs Saunders in Aberdeen went to William Gallagher of the Page's Hill kennel; some Eltham Park Champions from the kennels of Mr Pierce went to various other fanciers. In fact, the flow of top-quality Shelties going to the USA from the UK must have been considerable. There was no variance in type at that time between the two countries, so the difference now must be as a result of the show scene on either side of the Atlantic.

In the UK there are mostly specialist judges; in the US, all shows, except the Specialties, engage all-rounder judges. The breed has not always enjoyed an easy transition from Toonie or Peerie dog to leaning towards Collie-type. It is incredible to think how small they were when first brought to the mainland from the Shetland Isles, and size seems to have been a major stumbling block. It is recorded that specimens of 10 inches were being exhibited; gradually the size was increased and increased until the present Standard of an ideal of 14 inches for bitches, 14 and a half inches for dogs. A reasonable variance either side of the ideal is acceptable.

Many of the early kennels were very large and obviously had a great influence on the show ring by sheer force of numbers. Some of the first pillars of the breed when it was virtually feeling its way were probably Lerwick, owned by Mr Logie, Inverness, owned by Mr Thompson and Downfield, owned by Mr Ramsay.

Early in the 1920s, influential kennels were Kilravock, owned by Miss Thynne, Mountford, owned by Miss Humphries, Clerwood, owned by Dr Todd, and Peabody, owned by Mrs Montgomery. Possibly the most influential of all was Mrs Baker of the Houghton Hill affix. Mrs Campbell of the Tilford prefix was a generous and noteworthy breeder. Mr and Mrs Saunders of the Helensdale Shelties were known to favour the Collie type and advertised their kennels as such. Helensdales had showmanship and glamour, and with clever in-breeding, a type was soon established.

THE THIRTIES
During the 1930s, several kennels emerged that are still well-known today – the Callarts of Miss Gwynne Jones, Mrs Seys and the Inchmery kennels (though these now carry the prefix Rhodora). Mrs Sangster of the Exford affix was the daughter of the Houghton Hill breeder, and they must have been a formidable team!

The Misses Rogers started the Riverhills, and Bob Taylor formed the Wyndora kennel. In the North West, Mrs Fishpool formed her Ellington strain. Many kennels came into being, and the Sheltie seemed to be in a healthy state. The outbreak of World War II had a devastating effect, as many kennels had to be disbanded. The generosity of our friend in the USA, William Gallagher, was unique – he sent copies of the American handbook free of charge to be sold to members of the English Shetland Sheepdog Club, the monies helping to keep the Club funds solvent during those difficult times.

THE FORTIES
The 1940s saw an amazing number of people taking up the hobby of Sheltie breeding. There was Mrs Charlton in Hull with the Melvaig affix – these were founded on a Riverhill bitch, and though only a small family kennel, enjoyed considerable success. The Dryfesdale prefix, belonging to Eddie Watt in Scotland, started producing some lovely Shelties. Mr and Mrs Bellas Simpson started their Hallinwood kennel in South London. This was to be a large, very competitive kennel and I am always surprised that more has not been written about them. Mrs Greig of South Devon formed her small family kennel of Lydwell, while at the other end of England, Miss Heatley of Carlisle started off the Whytelaws, and she was one of the best handlers in the show ring. The Whytelaws built up a wonderful reputation which was to last many decades.

THE FIFTIES
The 1950s saw the formation of the largest kennel in the breed, which soon

Shelert Champions (left to right): Spice, Spark, Sweet Sultan, Sigurd, Midas and Shantung (all Of Shelert), showing the recognisable quality of this famous kennel.   *Photo: Unne.*

swept to the top and stayed in the number one position for many, many years. This was the Shelert kennel, owned by the Misses Herbert in North Yorkshire. Their first Shelties were actually Melvaigs, and in fact they enjoyed considerable success with Lyric and Jasper of Melvaig, the former winning two CCs. The foundation stones of the Shelert kennels were two Riverhill bitches – Royal Flush, who became their first Champion, and Rosalie, who is behind many Shelert pedigrees.

Also in Yorkshire, Mrs Charlesworth was building a strain mostly noted for tricolours and blue merles in her Dilhorne Shelties. She bred a dog, Ch. Dilhorne Blackcap, who was one of those 'dream' stud dogs producing winners to a variety of bitches – his stock were recognisable by their lovely heads.

The Francehill kennel was founded in the South of England by the then young Miss Bagot, and continues to breed and exhibit Shelties today. In London, Mrs Speding started her Antoc

Ch. Orpheus Of Callart (Hector Of Abelour – Heathbelle Of Callart): A Champion in 1950. Bred and owned by Miss O. Gwynne-Jones.

Bournemough Championship Show 1959. Pictured (left to right): The author with Mrs Harker's Ch. Gay Lass Of Melvaig, Miss P.M. Rogers (Riverhill) and Mr C.V. Smale with Ch. Penvose Brandy Snap.

kennel of Collies and Shelties, and while not actively showing Shelties nowadays, she remains one of our top judges. She was a most successful exhibitor in the 1950s and 1960s, gaining many CCs with the well known Ch. Antoc Sealodge Spotlight. Mrs Guest became a keen fancier of Shelties, starting with Hallinwood Sunset Gold, who produced the first of the Tooneytown Champions – Trumpeter of Tooneytown, a handsome shaded son of Ch. Alasdair of Tintobank.

In the Midlands, Mr and Mrs Jefferies founded their Jefsfire kennel of Collies and Shelties. Their foundation bitch became a Champion – Heathlow Luciana. She had been bred by Mrs Lowe, who had considerable success with her Heathlow stock. Luciana produced a son who was to earn a well-deserved place in Sheltie history – Ch. Jefsfire Freelancer. In Scotland, interest in Shelties seemed to wane somewhat, but a young man purchased Blue Girl of

Helensdale Frolic (Ch. Helensdale Bhan – Int. Ch. Helensdale Wendy): An influential sire of the 1950s. Bred by Mr and Mrs J. Saunders, owned by the author.

Ch. Trumpeter Of Tooneytown (Ch. Alasdair Of Tintobank – Hallinwood Sunset Gold). Bred and owned by Mrs M. Guest.

Exford, and this was the foundation for Albert Wight of the Sharval kennel in Edinburgh. This kennel was soon to make its mark. Only a few dogs were kept, but quality was always to the fore – the first Champion was Sharval Burlesque.

Another Scottish kennel just forming was Mr and Mrs Caldwell with their Monkreddan strain, who produced a string of lovely sable Champions. In the North East, Mr Henry added Shelties to his list of many interests, and being a stock-man through and through, he soon took his Greenscrees to the top. There was a great deal of interest in the breed in the North East; Mr Baker began his Ellendales, as did Mr and Mrs Craven of the Tyneford prefix. Miss Audrey Todd started her Sheldawyn Shelties – her first Champion was

Shadyfern of Sheldawyn, a pale golden sable daughter of Ch. Helensdale Ace.

Mr Smale from Cornwall founded his Penvose prefix on two Helensdale

Mrs Aileen Greig with two Lydwell puppies. This was a winning kennel of the 1950s.

Ch. Sharval The Delinquent (Carousel Of Melvaig - Sharval Cilla Black): Winner of 15 CCs - a one-time breed record. Bred and owned by Albert Wight.

Ch. Rockaround Blue Gamble (Surprise Packet Of Exford – Francehill Rollicking). Bred and owned by Mrs J. Angell.

bitches, and matings to Helensdale dogs produced some very successful Champions. A glamorous golden sable dog was Ch. Penovose Brandy Snap. In East Anglia Miss Blount, a Pembroke Corgi breeder, decided to add Shelties to her Rhinog prefix and produced many top winners. A Collie fancier was to come under the spell of the Sheltie and this was Mrs Goodwin, whose Hildlane kennel became famous, mostly for blue merles and tricolours. Another kennel in this area to form at about this time was Rockaround, founded by Mrs Angell on two Francehill bitches. Some of the Rockaround Champions were superb and her blue merles are behind many today.

THE SIXTIES
In the 1960s, there seems to have been an explosion in the breed's popularity and a lot of now-famous kennels were formed. Shelties were drawing large entries at the shows and the top kennel awards were keenly fought over. The Exfords, Riverhills and Shelerts were the leaders, and jealously guarded their positions at the top of the tree. A Collie breeder, Mr Frank Mitchell of the Glenmist kennels, bought a bitch from Riverhill and made her into a Champion – this was Riverhill Rarity of Glenmist. She, in turn, was a good brood bitch and produced Ch. Gipsy Star of Glenmist, while her litter sister produced Glenmist Golden Falcon, the sire of the top producer, Ch. Jefsfire

Freelancer. The Misses Davis returned to the UK from Switzerland, bringing with them Riverhill Rose Red, and it was possibly the purchase of Riverhill Rolling Home that put their Monkswood strain firmly on the road to success. Monkswood adhered closely to Riverhill lines and later produced the much admired Ch. Monkswood Moss Trooper. Mr and Mrs Tingley began their Stormane kennel of sables and they produced many winners. Starting with a Riverhill bitch, their first CC winner was Stormane Sherry, a top-quality bitch by Ch. Trumpeter of Tooneytown. I often wonder why she did not get her final CCs. However, many Champions were to follow bearing the Stormane prefix.

Mrs C. Sangster with Ch. Exford Pipestyle Mystic Star and Miss F.M. Rogers with Ch. Riverhill Richman: CC winners at Crufts and ESSC Championship Show 1969.

Mrs Joyce Seaman initially started her Joywil kennels in Yorkshire along Shelert lines. Noted for sables, the first homebred Champion was a beautifully headed red sable dog called Winston of Joywil. He had that stamp of quality, reminding me of his grandsire, Ch. Midas of Shelert. Janetstown is the prefix of Mrs Moody of Worcester. This prefix soon became synonymous with Shelties that were superbly presented for the show ring. The first homebred Champion was Janetstown Jacqualine, owned by Mrs Durose. Noted for sables, probably the best-known has been the glamorous Ch. Jack Point of Janetstown. Mrs Marshall was producing some consistent stock. Her prefix of Forestland was to become well-known, and built up a reputation for lovely movement. They have stood the test of time, and after producing a string of sable Champions over the decades, 1997 saw the crowning of the first blue merle, Ch. Forestland

Constance Sangster with a winning team of Exfords.

Ch. Jefsfire Freelancer (Glenmist Golden Falcon – Ch. Heathlow Luciana): Joint recordholding sire with 12 Champion progeny.

Emperor Moth, handled at most of the shows by Alison Lycett.

In Scotland Miss Susan Sangster, step-daughter of Mrs Sangster (Exford), was making progress with her Drumcauchlie Shelties. Although bred along Exford lines, this prefix was independent and had built up a fine reputation for soundness. The first Champion was Drumcauchlie Amethyst, a beautiful blue merle. The Loughrigg Shelties of Mrs Britten started with a quality tricolour, Faraway of Tooneytown, bred by Mrs Guest by Ch. Trumpeter of Tooneytown out of Ch. Christie of Tooneytown, proving that a good foundation bitch is worth her weight in gold. She produced many winners, including Ch. Loughrigg Dragon Fly. The Kyleburn prefix was formed by Mrs Eaves and it was soon apparent what a talented breeder she was, breeding many Champions, the first being Ch. Kyleburn Golden Eagle. I was a great admirer of this dog, in fact giving him his first CC. He features behind many of today's winners.

Not many people have the good fortune to make their foundation bitch a Champion, but this is just what Mr and Mrs Morewood did when they purchased Helensdale Vanessa. She was

Ch. Drumcauchlie Bumble Boy (Drumcauchlie Humourist – Drumcauchlie Bumble Bee). Bred and owned by Miss S. Sangster.

a golden sable and the last Champion to come from Mr and Mrs Saunder's kennel in Aberdeen. Mr and Mrs Morewood aimed to carry on the Helensdale line and bred Vanessa to my own Helensdale Frolic, the result being Ch. Sumburgh Sirius, the first of many Sumburgh Champions.

I first recall Mr Rigby of the Lythwood prefix in Shropshire, showing a blue merle in the mid-1960s, Lythwood Powder Puff. Since then, his kennels are mostly noted for sables, the first Champion was Lythwood Brandy Snap, and today Ch. Lythwood Skymaster is revered as one of the breed's great stud dogs. The Lythwoods have set a remarkable record of producing five homebred sable tail male Champions.

There can be few families so entrenched in the dog scene as the Gatheral family from Darlington. Colonel Gatheral was a well-respected all-breeds judge, and Mrs Gatheral bred Dalmatians. Luckily for the Sheltie world, Miss Mary Gatheral decided to add Shelties to the many breeds with which the family were having considerable success. I recall Miss Gatheral showing Riverhill Roquet and indeed lots of the 'of Herds' Shelties go back to him. Several Champions have been produced since – Ch. Herds

Ch. Deloraine Living Doll (Forestland Poacher – Ch. Deloraine China Doll). Bred by Mrs F. Chapman, owned by Mrs. J. Chater. Photo: Carol Ann Johnson.

Hurdler was one of my favourites. The present breed record holder is Ch. Herds the Helmsman, a glamorous golden sable and white.

Mrs Floss Chapman was a famed Collie breeder, her prefix of Deloraine was well known. Deciding to add Shelties to her kennel, she purchased a bitch of Antoc descent and mating her to Riverhill Rolling Home, she bred Deloraine Dilys of Monkswood, who was owned by Miss M Davis and Mrs E Knight and won a thrilling BoB at Crufts, topping that by annexing the working group. It was not until 1983 that her first owned and bred Champion was born – Deloraine China Doll, a blue merle. Sadly Mrs Chapman did not live to see the crowning of her final Champion, Deloraine Living Doll, who won her third CC under Miss Mary Crowley from Ireland, whilst in the proud ownership of Mrs Joan Chater.

Meanwhile in East Anglia a flurry of activity was taking place and several kennels started. Mrs Marriage of the Scylla affix was fortunate in purchasing Scylla Swan Princess of Callart, bred by Miss Gwynne Jones, and mated her to Ch. Dilhorne Blackcap. The result was a lovely tricolour bitch, Ch. Black Swan of Scylla. Mrs Marriage has achieved breeding champions in all three colours. The Felthorn prefix of Mr and Mrs Thornley began with the purchase of Francehill Pretty Polly, who was a litter sister to Ch. Francehill Silversmith,

both by Ch. Dilhorne Blackcap. Her grandson became their first Champion, Felthorn Beachcomber, and they too have also produced champions in all three colours. In fact they have the distinction of breeding four generations of tail female blue merle Champions, a feat not achieved before.

Although we tend to think of the Midnitesun kennel as being residents of Wales, the kennel was actually started when Mr and Mrs Wilbraham were living in Hertfordshire. The foundation bitch was Kyleburn Mignonette and she proved invaluable by producing Ch. Midnitesun Four Leaf Clover, who was one of my favourites.

The prefix of Shelridge, owned by Mrs Aaron, is also well-known. The foundation bitches were a Lysebourne and a Francehill. Although consistent winners were being produced, it was not until the 1980s that the first Champion appeared – Ch. Shelridge Ceilidh. She was five generations on from Francehill Cinderella, so that just shows how patience can pay off! Ch. Sheldridge Haywire won BoB at Crufts under Mrs Marriage in 1989.

THE SEVENTIES
During the early 1970s two sisters were to take the Sheltie world by storm with their Myriehewe kennel, then in Cheshire. Gwen and Irene Beaden soon established a type noted for showmanship. The first Champion was Merry Rustler of Myriehewe and many

146

Ch. Mountmoor Blue Boy (Ch. Longdells Petrocelli – Shelridge Carte Blance At Mountmoor) Winner of 15 CCs. Bred and owned by Mrs C. Ferguson and Miss E. Ford.

more have followed. There have been Champions in all three colours. The foundation bitches were Drannoc Flower Girl and Rodhill Elfin Moon, bred by Mrs Josie Rae. In the North East a small but competitive kennel was founded by Mrs McIntosh of the Shelderon prefix. The first Champion was a bright golden sable, Shelderon Gay Ghillie, who had a lovely head like so many of the progeny of Ch. Jefsfire Freelancer. The kennel was started with a Sumburgh bitch, therefore a strong Helensdale influence coming through. In later years blue merles and tricolours have taken precedence.

In the North West Mr and Mrs Fitzsimons formed their Snabswood strain, starting with a bitch of Ellington and Whytelaw descent – possibly why we associate this kennel with such good head and eye shape. The first of many Champions was Snabswood Slainthe. Throughout the years I have only seen sables with this prefix. From the same region of the country came the Sonymer shelties, owned by Mrs Ann Latimer and the late Mr Gordon Latimer. Ann is a well known personality in the breed – her experience is unique as she worked in the Whytelaw kennels before starting her own strain of Shelties. The foundation bitches were Whytelaw and Jefsfire. Strangely it was some years before the 'breakthrough' to top honours, Ch. Sonymer Sheena being the first Champion.

Also in the North West area, Mr and Mrs Bispham had taken a great fancy to

Ch. Herds Heatherbelle At Beckwith (Beckwith Bit Of A Maverick – Herds Harknow). Bred by Miss M. Gatheral, owned by Mr and Mrs D. MacMillan. Photo: MacMillan.

our breed and registered Bridgedale as their prefix. The foundation bitches were a Sumburgh and a Doshell and mated to Ch. Rodhill Burnt Sugar; the former produced a splendidly handsome sable dog which became their first Champion – Bridgedale Playboy.

Meanwhile in East Anglia, Mrs Ferguson bought a Francehill bitch and is one of those people who 'hit the jackpot', as in her first litter produced a Champion. This was Ch. Mountmoor Jeanie McCall. She was such a glamorous little bitch, being a bright red gold in colour and a great showgirl. The Mountmoors are owned in partnership with Miss Ford and have a keen interest in obedience as well.

In the London area a small kennel was taking shape owned by Mrs Moore. The Shetlo prefix produced a bitch which the English Shetland Sheepdog Club use as their blueprint for head, ears and expression, this being Ch. Shetlo Sheraleigh. She proved herself not only as a wonderful show dog, but by also producing a Champion son in Shetlo the Gay Piper, who was by Ch Rhinog the Gay Lancer. Also in the London area, later moving to the South of England, Mrs Crossley was campaigning her Willowtarn shelties. They were well known winners but the first Champion was a sable bitch bred by the Fitzsimons; Snabswood Summer Wine at Willowtarn. The first homebred champion was Willowtarn Telstar, a handsome shaded sable.

In the late 1970s a little sable dog entered the ring and won over many hearts. He was such a character and enjoyed the limelight of the show ring.

I first saw him as a puppy at the Scottish Shetland Sheepdog Club's Championship Show under the all-rounder, Harry Glover. This was Haytimer of Hanburyhill at Hartmere, bred by Mrs Archer of the Radash Shelties and Schipperkes, but owned by Rev and Mrs Hambrey, and Mr and Mrs M Hart. Haytimer soon gained his title and sired several Champions; he was the spearhead for the Hartmeres and several champions have since been produced. Mr and Mrs Hart have had the thrill of winning the CC at Crufts with two different bitches, Ch. Rainelor Reinetta and Ch. Hartmere Hello Gorgeous.

Mr and Mrs MacMillan from Yorkshire fell for the charms of the Sheltie and founded their Beckwith kennel. Several well-known winners were produced. The first Beckwith-bred Champion was the tricolour dog, a son of Ch. Herriot of Herds, Beckwith Bit of a Vagabond at Shelmyth, owned by Mrs Roseanna Smith. The first Champion campaigned by them was a little sable, Herds Heatherbelle at Beckwith, who was bred by Miss Gatheral, and by Beckwith Bit of a Maverick. Mr and Mrs MacMillan also bred the lovely Ch. Cultured at Cashella, owned by Mr and Mrs Johnstone.

Mrs Tunnicliffe with her Dippersmoor Shelties was residing in the West Midlands and founded her kennel on Allanvail Bitta Sweet at Dippersmoor. It is surprising that there are not a string of Champions bearing the Allanvail prefix because they were synonymous with quality. So the

Ch. Winston Of Joywil (Warwick Lad Of Joywil – Jewel Of Joywil). Bred and owned by Mrs Joyce Seaman.

Dippersmoors were lucky indeed to have this start – the first Champion was Dippersmoor Diester, a handsome shaded sable. He created a bit of a stir when he won his second CC as this was at the English Shetland Sheepdog Club Championship Show under Mrs Speding; his first CC was at this same show the previous year under Mrs Moody!

The Mohnesse kennel, also from the Midlands, was started by Mr and Mrs Greenhill, but very early on they had a lot of help from their daughter, Kay. The prefix soon became noted for glamorous golden sables and superb presentation was always a keynote. The first homebred Champion was Mohnesee Sweet Martini, a daughter of Ch. Francehill Persimon. She was soon followed by Mohnesee Sweet Reflection, who won her first CC in style at Crufts, under Albert Wight.

The remarkable thing about Miss Harrison of the Glaysdale prefix is that her success was achieved with one bitch! A keen enthusiast of obedience, the little tricolour bitch, Greensands Glad Eye was mated to Ch. Francehill Beach Boy, and the resulting litter produced the homebred Ch. Glaysdale Boy Wonder, a beautifully moving shaded sable. The next litter by Ch. Francehill Andy Pandy went one better, as Glad Eye produced two Champions! Glaysdale Heiress won her third CC at the Yorkshire Shetland Sheepdog Club Show, and Glaysdale Buccaneer also

won his third CC at the same Show on the same day. He was owned by Mrs I. Davidson. A truly remarkable achievement!

A quiet, unassuming person is Mrs Shovelton, who with her son Ian has made quite an impact on the Sheltie world. The first Champion was Ch. Dunbrae Gold n' Bianco of Diomed, who was owned by Mr & Mrs Richardson. Following this was Ch. Miss Mandy of Dunbrae at Faradale, who is owned by Mr & Mrs Jackson, and completing the hat-trick, making a Champion in all three colours, is Mrs Scott's Ch. Dunbrae Miss Dior of Penrave, a beautifully-coloured blue merle.

The later years of the 70s and early 80s saw several kennels emerge; the days of the large kennels seemed to wane, and instead many breeders took advantage of their foundation stock and started producing some lovely Shelties. One such kennel was Ceirrhig, owned by Mr and Mrs Griggs in West Yorkshire. The foundation bitch was Kyleburn Reed Warbler and she was the grandmother of the first Champion from this kennel, the tricolour dog, Ceirrhig Cragsman. He was a very handsome dog and won the CC and BoB at Crufts at the swan song of Miss Beryl Herbert's judging career in 1985. The purchase of Nitelife Rothschild brought Riverhill blood into the strain, the Ceirrhigs being a blend of Kyleburn and Riverhill.

Ch. Haytimer Of Hanburyhill At Hartmere (Ch. Riverhill Riccotta – Hanburyhill Honeysuckle): An influential sire of the 1980s. Bred by Mrs R. Archer, owned by Rev and Mrs Hambrey and Mr and Mrs Hart.

THE EIGHTIES

In the early 1980s a pair of brothers appeared in the show ring, one of which became a one-time record holder for the number of CCs. They were both beautiful dogs – the merle was Ch. Pepperhill Blue Fizz and his brother the tricolour, Pepperhill Gifted and Black. They were owned by Mrs Sorockyj but bred by Mrs Daniels of the Pepperhill prefix. Blue Fizz was a great ambassador for our breed, his presentation and showmanship were superb. Several Pepperhill Champions have followed, this time in the ownership of their breeder who is in partnership with Miss Taylor, and the prefix is well known for tricolours and blue merles, though a sable Champion has now been produced in Pepperhill Magic Dream with Mohnesee owned by Kay de Wilde. This makes Pepperhill the producers of Champions in three colours.

In East Anglia, Mrs Lyn French had already bred a Champion in Lirren Evening Shadow at Ramtin, a tricolour dog ably campaigned by his owner, Mrs Martin of the Ramtin prefix. Mrs French bought a sable bitch from Mr and Mrs Hart and had the thrill of making her into a Champion, Hartmere Hayday at Lirren, a daughter of Ch. Haytimer and Ch. Hebson Galeforce at Hartmere. Scylla Estella was purchased from Mrs Marriage and the Lirrens have bred several Champions, one of my favourites being the lovely Lirren Paper Moon, a daughter of Ch. C'ur C'in Fun Bug and Estella.

The Franwick Shelties started off with a Radash bitch and were soon producing quality stock; the first home-

Ch. Lirren Paper Moon (Ch. C'Ur C'In Fun Bug – Scylla Estella At Lirren). Owned and bred by Mrs L. French.

and she produced the first homebred Champion, a tricolour bitch named Gypsy of Rance. The next Champion was also a tricolour bitch, and what a charmer she was – Ladybird of Landover, bred down from Kyleburn lines. It was a granddaughter of hers, but by Ch. Swiftlight Otello which was the third tricolour bitch Champion for Mr. Perry, and this was Landover Bethan.

Meanwhile, also exponents of the Exford line were Mr and Mrs Hussey with the Nitelife prefix. Gill Hussey began with a daughter of a truly lovely bitch, Ch. Exford Pipestyle Mystic Star, namely Exford Solar Star. She was mated to Riverhill Ringsider and produced the first homebred Champion in Nitelife Rogue Star. He was a dog of great quality and one of his daughters was to become a Champion too. This was Nitelife Moon Shadow. We have already mentioned Nitelife Rothschild who, though not a Champion himself, did such a lot to contribute to the Ceirrhig kennel.

When Mr and Mrs Gibbens bought their first Sheltie, it was with obedience training in mind, so Shelridge Double Glow of Stornaway was purchased from Mrs Aaron. This little blue merle attracted many admirers to the breed; some of her progeny were winning in the show ring as well as in obedience. Ch. Silver Lady of Stornaway was the kennel's first Champion, a sound-moving blue merle that produced the

bred Champion was Franwick Sungod, a son of Ch. Haytimer. Mrs. Wendy Wickenden produced another Champion from the same bitch, but this time sired by the tricolour, Philhope Shoestring; Ch. Franwick Sister Jane. Next came a mother and daughter duo, both of which gained their titles – Franwick Esmeralda and her tricolour daughter, Franwick Magpie. After Magpie was born, the mother became the property of Miss Gatheral, and it was in her ownership that Esmeralda became a Champion.

Two kennels in Wales are our next feature: both had a leaning towards tricolours and both were founded on Exford lines. Mr Reg Perry founded his Landover kennel with Gleam of Exford

Ch. Francehill Goodwill (Ch. Glaysdale Bucaneer – Shelert Sands Of Time): 1985 Working Group winner: bred and owned by the author. Photo: MacMillan.

equally handsome Ch. Stornaway Star Spangled. The sable Ch. Stornaway Sally Brown won two of her CCs at the English Shetland Sheepdog Club Shows.

The Blenmerrow Shelties owned by Mr and Mrs Lambert started off with two Ravensbeck bitches, bred down from Riverhill lines. The first Champion was the shaded sable, Blenmerrow Brewmaster, a handsome son of Monkswood Master Plan. The next Champion was also a shaded sable, Blenmerrow Oak Apple, who was BoB at Crufts under Mrs Jeffries in 1987.

The Marnham shelties are the property of Mr and Mrs Pollard from the South of England. The first Champion was the red sable dog Marnham the Joker, who was a son of Ch Lythwood Sky Master. Reference will show him to have a Champion dam as well – in truth he made his title a year before his mother! She was Ch. Marnham Merry Maker, a golden sable daughter of Ch. Willowtarn Telstar. The Joker had a litter sister, owned by Mrs Tracy Gartland, Marnham Melady at Arcot and she also became a Champion, this time a year after her mother. The Marnhams are noted for lovely ear carriage and alert showmanship.

In East Anglia, Mr and Mrs Bray decided to add Shelties to their already existing kennel of Borzois. The foundation bitch was Francehill Very Black. Her daughter mated to Ch. Salroyds Buzzer produced the first Champion, a beautifully constructed tricolour dog, Longdell's Petrocelli. The blue merle, Rosdyke Pepperami at Longdells, bred by Mr and Mrs Peach, won his first CC under Mrs Anderson at Driffield. The shaded sable, Longdells Going for Gold gained his title to give this kennel the honour of

Ch. Myriehewe Moonshine (Ch. Merry Rustler Of Myriehewe – Rodhill Elfin Moon). Bred and owned by Miss G. Beaden.

Champions in three colours.

Another kennel in the East, in Lincolnshire is the Rosdyke kennel of Mr and Mrs Peach. The foundation bitch was Alwillans Blue Cinderella, bred by Mrs Coup from Derbyshire. The first Champion was a blue merle of lovely type and colour, Rosdyke Moonlight Shadow. In fact, it is for blue merles that we associate this kennel, and they have produced many merles of top quality. Mrs Peach is the co-ordinator of the Sheltie Rescue and has worked tirelessly for the Sheltie 'down on his luck'.

We have mentioned Ch. Beckwith Bit of a Vagabond at Shelmyth as being bred by Mr and Mrs MacMillan and owned by Mrs Roseanna Smith of the Shelmyth Shelties in Yorkshire, and in the same year her first homebred Champion was made up, this time a

golden sable by Ch. Hartmere Harris Tweed and out of Beckwith Be Little Be Good, namely Shelmyth Sweet Expression.

Also in Yorkshire the Penrave Shelties, owned by Mrs June Scott, began their strain with Francehill Spring Fancy, who produced a tricolour Champion son in Penrave Private Benjamin. He was owned and campaigned by Mrs Rowan. The first homebred and owned Champion for Mrs Scott was the tricolour bitch Penrave Penny Black, who won her first CC at Leeds under Mrs Joyce Seaman.

After Ch. Penrave Private Benjamin, the Rowancrest Shelties continued an excellent run. A lovely sable bitch Champion was next, Gold Illusion at Rowancrest and she produced two Champions, one in the ownership of Mr and Mrs Munro, Ch. Rowancrest

Just Simply Red, and the other owned by his breeders Mr and Mrs Rowan, Ch Rowancrest Regality, a shaded sable that gave all Sheltie fanciers a great thrill when he won the CC at Crufts under Mrs Anderson, and went on to runner-up in the working group under Albert Wight.

The Mid-West area saw the rare combination of a father and daughter duo – Mr Roy Pearson and Miss Debbie Pearson with their Edglonian Shelties. The first Champion was bred by Mrs Birtles out of Rhinog Rather Elegant by Edglonian Minstrel Boy of Newsprig, this was Ch. Our Barny of Edglonian. He pulled off a major triumph when he went BIS at the English Shetland Sheepdog Club's Jubilee Show under Mr Baker and myself. Interestingly the bitch CC winner, Ch. Glencharm Witches Brew of Melcette was a daughter of the same sire. Their first homebred Champion was Edglonian Rather Prity and she was also by Edglonian Minstrel Boy of Newsprig!

Mrs Wilson, an enthusiast from East Anglia purchased Felthorn Lady Luck at Morestyle from Mr and Mrs Thornley, and she became a Champion. A litter sister to Ch. Felthorn Lady, she proved a good foundation as the two subsequent Champion sable dogs are her descendants – the father and son, Morestyle Moonriver and Morestyle Monsoon. Mr and Mrs Miles enjoyed considerable success with Myriehewe Magic Moments at Milesend. He was an excellent stud dog and is behind most of the present day Milesends. They continue to win top honours, having won BoB at Crufts in 1998 under Miss Gwynne Jones with the homebred Ch. Milesend Stormwarden.

I feel that no review of the influential kennels of the 1980s would be complete without a mention of Mr and Mrs Stanley of the Tegwel prefix. This kennel is an offshoot of the Lythwood strain and they have achieved breeding several Champions for other people. The first Champion was Tegwel

Ch. Francehill Dollar Bid Of Lochkaren (Ch. Francehill Goodwill – Ch. Francehill Dolly Bird Of Lochkaren). Owned by Mr and Mrs K. Mottram.

Ch. Herds The Helmsman (Ch. Tegwel Wildways Of Sandwick – Herds Hot Gossip): Joint breed recordholder, winner of 34 CCs. Bred and owned by Miss M. Gatheral.

Photo: Carol Ann Johnson.

Smuggler at Myriehewe, and a dog that has earned himself a place in the history books – Ch. Tegwel Wild Ways of Sandwick, owned by Mr Chris Mayhew. At the time of writing Wild Ways is the top sire All Breeds in the Dog World Top Sire List. A truly wonderful achievement. Another Champion dog is Tegwel Toy Boy of Chrisarion, owned by Mrs Penwarne, and the bitch Tegwel Spring Breeze for Mr and Mrs Cushley in Northern Ireland.

THE NINETIES
This brings us up to date to the 1990s. Who can say which present-day kennel is going to be influential, but Shelties are having a wonderful decade. Two top winners are, firstly, the glamorous sable, Ch. Herds the Helmsman (a Wild Ways son), bred and owned by Miss Gatheral. He came out as a puppy to win his first CC under Mrs Phyllis Rigby at the Scottish Breeds – then went on to Best in Show. He is now the joint current breed record holder, having won 34 CCs. Then, Ch. Myriehewe Rosa Bleu won her first CC as a puppy at the North of Ireland Shetland Sheepdog Club under Mrs Fallas. Little did we realise what thrills we were all in for! Owned and bred by Miss Irene Beaden, Rosa Bleu is by Faradale Facination. Winning the CC at Crufts under Alan

Ch. Jackpoint Of Janetstown (Scylla So Blessed At Felthorn – Winter Jasmine Of Jontygray At Janetstown): Working Group winner 1991. Owned by Mrs J. Moody.
Photo: Anne Roslin-Williams.

Jefferies, we cheered her on to win the working group; then, winning many CCs in-between, she won the CC at Crufts the following year under Mr Joe Kirk and repeated her win in the working group. Rosa Bleu is at present the joint record holder of 34 CCs.

Current winning kennels are Lythwood, Milesend, Herds, Myriehewe, Hartmere, Mohnesee, Dippersmoor, Felthorn, Shelridge, Pepperhill, Shelderon, Snabswood, Edglonian and Rannerdale.

Moving North over the border to Scotland consistently winning kennels are Orean, Harribrae, Japaro and Sommerville. Shows are still attracting large entries – the 1970s and 1980s saw the largest numbers entered at our Championship Shows, no doubt increased entry fees and the cost of travelling have deterred some otherwise keen Sheltie exhibitors!

157

13 THE SHELTIE IN NORTH AMERICA

BY SUE ANNE BOWLING

The modern British Shetland Sheepdog and the modern American Shetland Sheepdog are different enough that a British dog will rarely win over good American dogs under an American judge, and vice versa. The difference, however, is subtle; nothing like the difference between the American Cocker Spaniel and the English Cocker Spaniel.

This difference is due to a combination of several factors. For one, there are in fact slight differences in the Standards in the two countries. Shows are run somewhat differently in the two countries, which puts emphasis on different traits (such as showmanship). This in turn leads to breeders putting emphasis on different traits, and differing in how the Standard should be interpreted. Finally, and perhaps most importantly, the American Shetland Sheepdog is derived from a rather small fraction of the genetic material available in the UK. In particular, the influence of Ch. Blaeberry of Clerwood and the possible Collie cross Ashbank Glitter is overwhelming in North America, and importations after the first wave between 1929 and 1936 have had surprisingly little effect on the overall gene pool in North America. As one indication of this, Ch. Nicky of Aberlour (and his grandson Ch. Helensdale Ace) have almost no influence on the modern American Shetland Sheepdog.

HISTORY OF AMERICAN LINES

The American lines of today are derived primarily from the dogs imported, most by Anahassitt Kennels, in the early 1930s. Only one import since World War II has had any real influence on the breed in the United States, and that dog, like the early imports, was heavily linebred on the Chestnut cross. The letters ROM following a dog's name mean Register of Merit, and indicate that a dog has sired 10 or more US

158

Am. Ch. Toven Wintertide: Bred by Toni Mapes and Lorraine Bohmiller. Owned by Toni Mapes.   *Photo: Onaka Dudley.*

Champions, or a bitch has produced five or more.

ANAHASSITT
Mrs. Dreer of Anahassitt imported a number of Shetland Sheepdogs between 1929 and 1933. The most important of the dogs were US Ch. Wee Laird o'Downfield (Ch. Blaeberry of Clerwood x Downfield Ethne); US Ch. Dancing Master of Anahassitt (Ch. Uam Var of Houghton Hill x Ballet Girl of Houghton Hill), US. Ch. Bodachan of Clerwood (Ch. Euan of Clerwood x Bracken of Clerwood) and Sprig of Houghton Hill (Ch. Uam Var of Houghton Hill x Chestnut Garland). Her most important bitch imports were US Ch. Ashbank Fairy (Ch. Blaeberry of Clerwood x Ashbank Sheila), US Ch. Downfield Grethe (Ch. Blaeberry of Clerwood x Downfield Ethne) and

Natalie of Clerwood (Ch. Blaeberry of Clerwood x No No Nanette).

These seven dogs make up approximately 65% of the breeding behind the modern American Sheltie. Note that four of these Shelties were sired by Ch. Blaeberry of Clerwood, three being out of full sisters in blood. Two others were sired by Ch. Uam Var of Houghton Hill (one out of a Blaeberry daughter), another dog inbred on the Chestnut cross. The connection is a little more distant behind Ch. Bodachan of Clerwood, but Ch. Blaeberry of Clerwood was Bodachan's double-great-grandsire, while Chestnut Blossom (Blaeberry's dam) was his double-great-grandam.

Catherine Coleman of Sheltieland had

Mrs Dreer with import Ch. Bodachan Of Clerwood and homebred Ch. Gigolo Of Anahassitt who took Best of Breed at the second ASSA National Specialty.

started breeding in the US with Kilravock Lassie, a full sister to Chestnut Rainbow, a few years before the Anahassitt importations. While she imported a number of dogs over the years, the greatest part of her breeding came from the Anahassitt imports. One example of particular interest to the Sheltie world was US Ch. Sheltieland Laird o'Page's Hill. Although this dog traced tail female to Kilravock Lassie (five generations back), his sire was Ch. Mowgli ROM (Page's Hill from Anahassitt stock) and the remainder of his pedigree traced entirely to US Ch. Wee Laird o'Downfield and Natalie of Clerwood. He was sent to James

Am. Ch. Wee Laird O' Downfield (import) with son Anahassit's Ane Wee Laird.

Am. Ch. Mountaineer O'Page's Hill ROM.

Saunders in Scotland, and bred there to Balmedie Juno to produce Helensdale Biddy. His influence beyond that point is clear to see in the British charts for Family 1 part II – and note that the family chart does not include the influence of his descendant, Ch. Alasdair of Tintobank.

Mrs Dreer's health was not good, but she provided foundation stock to a number of other kennels. Two were of critical importance, producing the most important sires of the period before World War II: Page's Hill and Pocono.

PAGE'S HILL
Page's Hill was originally founded by William Gallagher, but was run for many years by the man who had

selected the Wee Laird, Natalie and Grethe for Mrs Dreer: J Nate Levine. The early breeding program at Page's Hill involved descendants of those three dogs, plus a daughter of the Wee Laird and US Ch. Ashbank Fairy, Anahassitt April Lady ROM. In general the Page's Hill dogs were tightly linebred on the Blaeberry offspring and were noted for their head qualities and elegance. Later direct imports to Page's Hill included US Ch. Rob Roy of Page's Hill and two Canadian sisters, Alford Heatherbloom and Alford Miss Heatherbelle. Both of the Canadian bitches were heavily linebred on Nan of Mountfort (Ch. Nettle of Mountfort x Monagard [Family 12]), who had been sent from Great Britain to Canada with several of her offspring.

US Ch. Mowgli ROM (19 Chs), the first US dog to sire over 10 US Champions, was the result of breeding US Ch. Wee Laird o'Downfield to his own daughter out of Downfield Grethe, Jean of Anahassitt. From very closely related bloodlines with the addition of Natalie of Clerwood and UK/US Ch. Rob Roy of Page's Hill, Page's Hill also produced China Clipper o'Page's Hill ROM (10 Chs) and US Ch. Mountaineer o'Page's Hill (22 Chs) – three of the first six Shelties who sired ten or more US Champions. A fourth producer of Champions, and in the long run the most influential, was China Clipper's littermate, US Ch. Kalandar Prince o'Page's Hill. This dog sired eight US Champions, two of which between them sired 45 US Champions. The pedigree of US Ch. Mountaineer o'Page's Hill is included as an example of the type of pedigree Page's Hill produced. It should be noted that there is some suspicion of Collie crosses in the apparently tightly inbred Page's Hill stock, with Jean of Anahassitt and US Ch. Kim o'Page's Hill being most often mentioned as Collie crosses.

POCONO

Pocono was founded by Elizabeth Whelen, who originally purchased an Anahassitt bitch, US Ch. Syncopating Sue of Anahassitt (US Ch. Dancing Master of Anahassitt x Anahassitt Atalanta ROM, the latter being a full sister of Anahassitt April Lady ROM). Betty imported a male of her own: US

Am. Ch. Larkspur Of Pocono CDX, ROM.

Ch. Peabody Pan (Peabody Paulet x Peabody Plume). Pan is second only to the Wee Laird in the influence of imports on the modern US Sheltie, accounting for about 11% of the modern American gene pool. The mating of Pan with Syncopating Sue produced US Ch. Merrymaker of Pocono CD ROM, the first US male to sire 25 Champions and one of the first high quality small males. US Ch. Peabody Pan was also heavily linebred on the Chestnut cross, and had Ch. Blaeberry of Clerwood as his great grandsire. The Pocono dogs were among the first to be involved with the then-new sport of obedience, and the kennel produced a truly extraordinary bitch in the blue merle Ch. Larkspur of Pocono CDX ROM, the dam of no less than sixteen Champions! The Pocono dogs were generally noted for relatively stable temperaments and good structure. The line was also much more loosely bred than were the Page's Hill dogs.

Pocono breeding also produced the other three of the first six sires of ten or more Champions: Pan's son Ch. Merrymaker of Pocono CD ROM (25 Chs), Merrymaker's son Ch. Merry Meddler of Pocono CDX ROM (21 Chs) and Meddler's son US Ch. Bil-Bo-Dot Blue Flag of Pocono ROM (14 Chs). Blue Flag's pedigree is included as an example of the looser breeding typical of Pocono.

TIMBERIDGE

1942 saw a historic cross between the Pocono and Page's Hill strains. Dot Foster of Timberidge had earlier borrowed Pandora of Pocono (US Ch. Peabody Pan x Astolat Lady Harlequin [bred by Pocono from Anahassitt lines]) for a litter by US Ch. Merrymaker of Pocono CD ROM. She then bred a lovely bitch from this pure Pocono litter, US Ch. Timberidge Temptress, to the Page's Hill sire, US Ch. Kalandar Prince o' Page's Hill (8 Chs). The litter included two sable males that are direct male descent to virtually every Sheltie in the United States today: US Ch. Timberidge Temptation ROM (32 US Champions, the record until the 60s) and US Ch. Prince George o'Page's Hill ROM (13 US Champions).

The next important step from both of these dogs involved another British import. This time the dog was UK/US Ch. Catmore Chum, and from Felicity Rogers' book on the breed, he was sent to the US in part for safety during World War II. Whatever the reason, he was mated to Indigo of Pocono, producing a tricolor bitch called Shelt-E-Ain Pirouette. Pirouette was mated to Ch. Timberidge Temptation ROM, the result being a sable male, Shelt-E-Ain Little Sir Echo, who was mated back to his dam to produce two very important Shelties: the tricolor dog Am Ch. Shelt-E-Ain Black Knight and the sable bitch, Nashcrest Rhythm. Black Knight, mated to another Pirouette daughter,

Am. Ch. Timberidge Temptation ROM.

produced US Ch. Shelt-E-Ain Reflection o'Knight ROM, who went to Pocono where he headed a new Pocono sire line, this one tracing to Ch. Blaeberry of Clerwood rather than to Ch. Gawaine of Cameliard.

US. CAN. CH. NASHCREST GOLDEN NOTE ROM

Temptation's littermate, US Ch. Prince George o'Page's Hill, did not at first appear to be any real competition for his brother. He seems to have been only lightly promoted by Page's Hill, and sired far fewer litters than Temptation's 129. So far as I have been able to learn, no photograph was ever taken once he was out of puppyhood. He was, however, mated to Nashcrest Rhythm, producing US/Can Ch. Nashcrest

163

Am. Ch. Sheltieland Kiltie O' Sea Isle (left) with mate Am. Ch. Sea Isle Summer Breeze (right) and daughter Am. Ch. Sea Isle Sandra (centre). Sandra bred to Note produced the dam of Am. Ch. Sea Isle Serenade.

Golden Note ROM. This dog heads what is by far the most important sire line in American Shelties today. He was sold to Sea Isle Kennels (Mary van Wagenen and Evelyn Davis), where he turned out to nick extraordinarily well with daughters of another dog the ladies of Sea Isle had obtained from Sheltieland, US Ch Sheltieland Kiltie o'Sea Isle.

Kiltie was deliberately linebred on one of Mrs. Dreer's imports, US Ch. Bodachan of Clerwood, and Bodachan's importance in modern pedigrees comes primarily through Kiltie. Kiltie's paternal grandsire, US Ch. Victory of Pocono CDX, was pure Pocono; his maternal grandsire, US Ch. Mountaineer o'Page's Hill ROM, was pure Page's Hill. His maternal grandam was bred on the West Coast with repeated crosses to Page's Hill males, while his paternal grandam combined an import not yet mentioned, Glenisla Elegance, who was also linebred on the Chestnut cross, with Page's Hill lines. The ladies of Sea Isle felt that his full muzzle, head planes, and ears were

Am. Ch. Sundowner Mr Bojangles CD, ROM.

Am. Ch. Macdega The Piano Man ROM: Top bi-colour sire in the US.
Photo courtesy: Tom Coen.

outstanding, but that he lacked coat and showmanship. These qualities, however, Note had in abundance. Many of the outstanding dogs produced by Sea Isle were based on breeding Note to Kiltie daughters.

The only other British import to have a widespread influence on the modern American Sheltie comes in at this point. In the 1950s, the Jacobs of Oak-Lawn kennels imported US Ch. Rocket of Exford (Jack Tar of Exford 1337AF x Ch. Bonfire of Exford 247AD), a dog who went back almost entirely to the original Houghton Hill lines, based on Nut of Houghton Hill. Bred to the Oak-Lawn bitches, Rocket was behind two important bitches who produced well to Kiltie. His daughter US Ch. Lochelven's Caprice produced US Ch. Lochelven's Reverie, who was bred to Kiltie to produce US/Can Ch. Colvidale Soliloquy.

Rocket was also the double great-

Am. Ch. Macdega Glenhart Grand Prix ROM: Sire of over 40 US Champions.
Photo courtesy: Tom Coen.

grandsire of another bitch bred to Kiltie: Miss Ruffles of Oak-Lawn. This mating produced US Ch. Kawartha's Sabrina Fair ROM, the dam (by Kiltie) of US Ch. Kawartha's Fair Game ROM and of US Ch. Kawartha's Match Maker ROM, the foundation sire at Mar Jan kennels. Unfortunately Match Maker, like his sire Kiltie and his great grandsire Mountaineer, tended to produce outstanding brood bitches rather than outstanding sires. His sire line, and the entire line coming through US Ch. Peabody Pan, is currently dormant in the direct male line, the last US Champion coming down from Pan having finished in 1990. This is a considerable shift, as some 20 years earlier Pan was responsible for about 30% of US Champions.

Note carries on today through two of his sons, US Ch. Lingard Sealect Bruce ROM and US Ch. Sea Isle Serenade ROM. Bruce was the first Sheltie to surpass Temptation's record of 32 Champions, winding up with 46 Champions to his credit. His most important son was US Ch. Diamond's Robert Bruce (out of a bitch who was linebred on Temptation and also a great granddaughter of Note). Robert Bruce sired both 'Pow' (Am/Can Cherden Sock It To 'Em ROM) and US Ch. Tentagel David Copperfield, sire of US Ch. Sundowner Mr. Bojangles CD ROM. A good deal of the bi-black (black and white) breeding in the US today traces to Pow and Bojangles,

though there is good reason to believe in both cases that the recessive black gene came through the dams rather than from Robert Bruce.

Another and more important son of Note started with the breeding of Note to the Kiltie daughter, US Ch. Sea Isle Sandra. This mating produced US Ch. Sea Isle Serenata who, mated back to her sire, produced US Ch. Sea Isle Serenade ROM, sire of 29 Champions. Serenade in turn sired two sons who carry on the line to modern Shelties: US Ch. Diamond's Redbud and US Ch. Malpsh the Duke of Erle.

Redbud was the result of mating Serenade to US Ch. Diamond's Black Velvet, the dam of US Ch. Diamond's Robert Bruce ROM. His main contribution today comes through the fact that his son, Ch. Tentagel Mr President CDX, was mated to a triple-great-granddaughter of US Ch. Halstors Peter Pumpkin ROM (probably the most important of the Serenade descendants) to produce US Ch. Chenterra Thunderation ROM. Thunderation was an extremely important dog in the 70s, and was the second Sheltie to exceed 200 Best of Breed wins, becoming for a while the top winner in breed history with 220 Best of Breed placings. He sired 24 US Champions, including one Register of Merit sire in US Ch. Macdega Mainstay ROM. Most of his current influence comes through two non-ROM sons, US Ch. Harvest Hills Final Word and

Can Ch. Ridgeside Star Wars. It may be of some interest that some of his semen was frozen, and he currently (1998) has offspring of only about a year old.

US Ch. Malpsh the Duke of Erle brought in a different bitch line. His dam, Sea Isle Dusky Belle, combined a Kiltie daughter, Bagaduce Hannah of Sea Isle, with US Ch. Pixie Dell Bright Vision, who was predominantly of Page's Hill lines. The mating of Dusky Belle with Serenade produced not only the Duke of Erle, but two non-champion producers as well: Malpsh Her Royal Madjesty ROM (5 Chs including a Register of Merit sire) and Pris ROM (5 Champions). The Duke of Erle himself sired nine Champions, but in addition, he sired a non-champion from whom the majority of US Shelties today descend tail male: Fair Play of Sea Isle ROM.

FAIR PLAY OF SEA ISLE ROM
Fair Play's dam was US Ch. Kawartha's Fair Game ROM, mentioned previously as a descendant of US Ch. Rocket of Exford.

US/Can Ch. Colvidale Soliloquy, mentioned above as a Rocket descendant, was also mated to Serenade, the result being US/Can/Bda Ch. Sea Isle Rhapsody of Halstor. When Rhapsody was mated to Fair Play, the result was a dog who today makes up close to 30% of the average US Sheltie pedigree: US Ch. Halstors Peter Pumpkin ROM, whelped in

1965. This dog sired 160 Champions (10 of whom earned the Register of Merit) to become the top producing Sheltie sire in US history. He also had over a hundred Best of Breed wins, won twice at the American Shetland Sheepdog Association National Specialty, and was an all-breed Best in Show dog. He was used in outcrossing, linebreeding, and frank inbreeding. and it is possible to find a dog who does not even show Peter in a four to five generation pedigree but who is half Peter by blood.

Nor was Peter the only great sire produced by Fair Play. Peter was mated to a bitch of basically Sea Isle lines, Beltane Holly Golightly, to produce Beltane High Barbaree. High Barbaree was then mated back to her sire, Peter, producing US Ch. Beltane Romayne. Romayne was mated back to her grandsire and great grandsire, Fair Play, to produce US Ch. Romayne's Sportin' Life ROM, the sire of 56 Champions including three Register of Merit sires.

BANCHORY
While Sea Isle lines (in the broad sense) were dominating over much of the country, a new kennel, Banchory, was making waves in the Pacific Northwest. The founding bitches came from a number of lines. Initially, Donna Langness bred this wide range of bitches to outside sires, with particular emphasis on US Ch. Thistlerose Arcwood Aladdin (US/Can Ch. Blue

Am. Can. Ch. Banchory High Born.

Quest of Pocono x US Ch. Thistlerose Classic Moderne ROM). She also leased US Ch. Philidove Heir Presumptive ROM, breeding him to outside bitches as well as to the stock she had bred to that point.

Heir Presumptive was a relatively outcrossed dog. His sire, US Ch. Heir Apparent of Karelane, was a son of US Ch. Blue Heritage of Pocono ROM, who combined US Ch. Shelt-E-Ain Reflection o'Knight ROM with Pocono-based breeding through Shelcourt and additional Temptation through Katie-J lines. His dam, Wansor's Flashy Flame, was of Astolat breeding: basically Page's Hill with some infusion of Temptation. Rosemary Shrauger bred her bitch, Tiree Hall Solo's High-Light, to Heir Presumptive. High-Light was herself outcrossed, her sire, Badgerton Wit o'Meadow Ridge, being more or less in the Sea Isle family (Note - Kiltie with some additional Timberidge) while her dam, Ch Lochindaal Solo of Tiree Hall, was primarily of Timberidge background. The common factor throughout the pedigree was Ch. Timberidge Temptation ROM, who made up around 15% of the total pedigree.

Donna (by then Donna Olson) obtained US Ch. Banchory High Born ROM from this breeding and used him on the bitches she had by that point accumulated, as well as offering him at public stud. Donna became Donna Tidswell in the early 70s, and around that time High Born went to Guy and Thelma Mauldin of Kismet Kennels. By then Donna had a number of High Born offspring, and had purchased a second dog she considered outstanding, US Ch. Cherden Sock It To 'Em CD ROM. 'Pow', as this dog was called, was the result of mating US Ch. Diamond's Robert Bruce ROM to a bitch linebred on US Ch. Thistlerose Arcwood Aladdin and Donna's foundation stock. He was used on many of the bitches coming down from High Born. In addition, Donna bred to several outside stud dogs, the most important being US Ch. Halstors Peter Pumpkin ROM and US Ch. Sundowner Mr. Bojangles CD ROM.

Bojangles was a dog whose sire was inbred Robert Bruce and whose dam

168

combined E-Danha (Page's Hill and Pocono), Page's Hill via Pixie Dell, Kiltie relatives, and old Noralee-Timberidge-west coast lines.

Eventually, this mixture produced no fewer than 11 Register of Merit sires. probably the most important of which was Banchory Reflection ROM, the result of mating High Born to his own daughter, Banchory High Glow.

High Glow actually produced well to several sires: Ch. Banchory the Cornerstone CD ROM, Ch. Banchory the Candidate and Ch. Banchory Arabesque to US Ch. Halstors Peter Pumpkin ROM, and Ch. Banchory Gypsy Queen to Pow. Two of her offspring, Banchory Reflection ROM and Ch. Banchory Arabesque, were mated to produce Ch. Banchory Formal Notice ROM, one of the outstanding dogs prematurely lost to the breed as a result of the "Banchory scandal" of the early 80s.

An ownership dispute threw up evidence suggesting puppies had been incorrectly registered, and an AKC investigation followed.

Subsequently Donna and Clare Harden were permanently barred from all AKC activities, including the showing and selling of dogs.

As one result, many outstanding dogs owned at the time by the Hardens were lost to the breed in America. As another, all Banchory pedigrees were called into question.

The unfortunate fact is that this question about Banchory pedigrees affects most of the Shelties in the United States today.

Neither Banchory nor Sea Isle still exists as a breeding kennel, but the predominant lines in the US are based on Sea Isle or Banchory foundations, or most often on both.

IMPORTANT BLOODLINES
If we take the Register of Merit dogs as an example of the most important bloodlines in the United States today, the Fair Play sons dominate among sables, while High Born and Robert Bruce have considerable influence among blacks and blues.

All of the current ROM sires trace tail male to US Ch. Banchory High Born ROM, US Ch. Chenterra Thunderation ROM, US Ch. Diamond's Robert Bruce ROM, US Ch. Halstors Peter Pumpkin ROM, or US Ch. Romayne's Sportin' Life ROM, all tracing to the Kalandar Prince x Temptress litter. High Born's line is the modern line from US Ch. Timberidge Temptation; the other four lines trace to US Ch. Prince George o'Page's Hill.

In general, the best dogs derived from Sea Isle breeding have very sweet expressions and heavy coats. They tend to mature slowly, and a Sea Isle Sheltie may not be ready to show before three or four years of age. Once they do mature, they hold quality into old age. A Sea Isle puppy that looks mature at a year old will probably go off and

Am. Ch. Halstor's Peter Pumpkin ROM: Sire of 160 US Champions.
Photo courtesy: Tom Coen.

become overdone with age. Some Sea Isle lines tend toward short necks, one of the few faults brought in by Peter.

Banchory lines are noted more for head planes and outline, including strong underjaws. They frequently have wider backskulls than do the Sea Isles, and sometimes lack coat or appear to have a harder expression. Banchory stock generally matures early, and do well as puppies, but a puppy who looks very mature is less likely to go off in the Banchory line. Both lines can vary widely in structure and movement.

In practice, there are kennels that are nearly pure Sea Isle and will not knowingly breed to Banchory stock, kennels which are basically linebred Fair Play but have a little Banchory breeding (often through US Ch. Banchory

Am. Ch. Romayne's Sportin' Life, owned by Tatsuko and George Danforth.

Formal Notice ROM), kennels which cross one or both of the lines with their own earlier stock, and a few kennels that focus on the lines coming from Banchory. A few pedigrees of Register of Merit dogs, as well as some recent ROM sire lines, are included and illustrate how the lines are being combined today.

CANADA

Shelties in Canada got their start with the importation of Nan of Mountfort (Ch. Nettle of Mountfort x Monagard), together with her daughters Sable Naneen (by Nip, both parents Chestnut Rainbow x Blue Floss of Houghton Hill), Wizbang Godiva (by Ch. Specks of Mountfort) and an in utero

*Banchory Reflection ROM.
Photo courtesy: Tom Coen.*

granddaughter, Can Ch. Wizbang Joy (by Ch. Gawaine of Cameliard). A Gawaine son was also imported, Wizbang Easter Hero (Gawaine x Ros Mairl, she by Bruce of Halstead ex Roseberry), while a second dog, Ch. Marbles of Greyhill (Moorman of Greyhill x Alley Tor) brought in the old Lerwick Jarl (LJA) line which survived at least into the late 30s in Canada. The Alford kennels were founded on these dogs, with crosses to Page's Hill stock from the United States.

After World War II, several Canadian kennels were formed, based primarily on the old Alford stock with crosses to both Page's Hill and Pocono dogs. Canada also continued to import dogs from the UK to a greater extent than did the USA. Modern Canadian lines, however, have been crossed so much with the Sea Isle and Banchory strains that there is little influence of the original Canadian stock. One post-war import to Canada who has made it into modern pedigrees is Hallinwood Skylon, a son of Ch. Helensdale Ace ex Hallinwood Elegance.

COMPARING STOCK

While selection and history played a large role in the difference between US and British Shelties, the differences in foundation stock still need to be considered. With modern computers it is possible to calculate the fraction of a particular pedigree contributed by any given dog, allowing 50% for a parent, 25% for each time as a grandparent, and so on, as well as how many times a dog occurs behind another dog. These calculations have been carried out for several key dogs in early Sheltie history: Chestnut Sweet Lady, Teena, Ashbank Glitter, Ch. Blaeberry of Clerwood, and Nut of Houghton Hill. In general the results were much more variable for British dogs than for those bred in America and derived mostly from the limited early imports. Specifically: Chestnut Sweet Lady contributes 10% to 20% to the British Sheltie; 20% to the US Sheltie. Teena contributes 4% to 8% to the British Sheltie; 4% to the US Sheltie. Ashbank Glitter (a dog whose pedigree was considered suspect and possibly Collie by other breeders of the day) contributes about 2.5% to the British Sheltie but a whopping 13% to the US Sheltie. Ch. Blaeberry of Clerwood contributes 10% to the British Sheltie, but 31% in the United

States. Nut of Houghton Hill, the main conduit of the CHE line in Great Britain, contributes 10% to 20% to the British Sheltie and only 4% to 5% in the United States. Finally, to show the difference in Helensdale influence, Ch. Nicky of Aberlour, who averages around 20% influence in Great Britain (38% in Ch. Helensdale Ace) rarely exceeds a tenth of a percent in the US.

As far as numbers are concerned, dogs with over a million crosses to Teena in their pedigrees are not uncommon in the US, and the same is true of Chestnut Sweet Lady. Hundreds of thousands of crosses are typical for Blaeberry, Glitter and Nut. This, however, is mainly an effect of how far back these dogs are in modern pedigrees.

For students of the line and family charts, US Champions are almost entirely in Line CHE, and current Champions are in the part of Line CHE derived from Chestnut Lucky Boy. The dominant family in the US is Family 2 through Ashbank Jean. Other important Families are 5 (through Helensdale Lassie), 6 (through No No Nanette, a daughter of Netherkeir Nan) and 12 (through Nan of Mountfort.)

US Ch. Banchory Sis O'Browne Acres and her full sister Browne Acres Bewitching combined Page's Hill via Pixie Dell with Timberidge lines. Lodgewood Chip of Cloudmere was basically Pocono by pedigree, a daughter of US Ch. Blue Heritage of

Am. Ch. Lakehill King O' The Road.   *Photo: Krook.*

Pocono. She produced two bitches who went to Banchory, Lodgewood Sonata ROM and Lodgewood Queen o'Banchory. Briarwood Bells-A-Ringing was Sea Isle breeding. Another foundation bitch was US Ch. Carmylie Lady Fair, a granddaughter of US Ch. Kawartha's Fair Game. Still another was Scothill Jody of Misty Dawn, who was three quarters Thistlerose (predominantly derived from Timberidge). Lodgewood Scherzo again traced primarily to Pocono lines. Brandwyne Sugar Blue combined Pocono lines with Astolat and Pixie Dell. Carmylie Bliss o'Banchory combined Sea Isle and Badgerton with Am Ch. Kawartha's Fair Game ROM.

Thistlerose lines were based on Ch. Timberidge Tempatation ROM with additions from both Page's Hill and Pocono.

Am. Ch. Lynnlea's Playing With Fire: Winners Bitch and Best of Winners at the 1998 ASSA Specialty.

14 *FINAL NOTE*

Having completed the enjoyable task of writing this book, I would like to close with a few reminiscences.

Nothing can compare with the devotion which your Sheltie has given you. If you are a pet owner, then you will have enjoyed each other's company, and I am willing to bet that no other member of the family has given you such unconditional love. I recall a charming couple collecting their puppy and on leaving I was taken aside by the husband, who smilingly said that now he had his 'true love' tucked under his arm!

If you are a keen exhibitor, try to accept wins, or losses, with grace and modesty – after all, the judge is only doing his or her job and it might be your turn to officiate soon! How embarrassing for the Sheltie who once saw his owner tear up his well-earned second place prize card!

If you are the owner of a kennel, I hope there have been some useful tips in the book which will help you continue on the road to success. Try to remain patient when that single voice on the phone arrives to view your puppies, accompanied by Granny, Auntie, next door neighbours and all their children, on a rainy day!

In whatever way we have become attracted to these wonderful little dogs, it remains the duty of us all to love and care for them to the best of our ability. Whether a mere human or a Sheltie, a little praise is always appreciated. I remember completing a mammoth judging appointment at one of our major Championship Shows, and on packing up at the end of the day, I was confronted by a dear old lady: "Eeh, Luv, you 'ave done well…" I glowed – how nice to have some praise, only to hear her final remark, "You must 'ave a bladder like a camel"!